Development Centr

C000057817

Policy Ownership and Aid Conditionality in the Light of the Financial Crisis

A CRITICAL REVIEW

OECD

ORGANISATION FOR ECONOMIC CO-OPERATION AND DEVELOPMENT

The OECD is a unique forum where the governments of 30 democracies work together to address the economic, social and environmental challenges of globalisation. The OECD is also at the forefront of efforts to understand and to help governments respond to new developments and concerns, such as corporate governance, the information economy and the challenges of an ageing population. The Organisation provides a setting where governments can compare policy experiences, seek answers to common problems, identify good practice and work to co-ordinate domestic and international policies.

The OECD member countries are: Australia, Austria, Belgium, Canada, the Czech Republic, Denmark, Finland, France, Germany, Greece, Hungary, Iceland, Ireland, Italy, Japan, Korea, Luxembourg, Mexico, the Netherlands, New Zealand, Norway, Poland, Portugal, the Slovak Republic, Spain, Sweden, Switzerland, Turkey, the United Kingdom and the United States. The Commission of the European Communities takes part in the work of the OECD.

OECD Publishing disseminates widely the results of the Organisation's statistics gathering and research on economic, social and environmental issues, as well as the conventions, guidelines and standards agreed by its members.

ISBN 978-92-64-07551-1 (print)
ISBN 978-92-64-07552-8 (PDF)

ISSN 1563-4302 (print)
ISSN 1190-0295 (online)

Also available in French: *Appropriation et conditionnalité de l'aide : Une revue critique à la lumière de la crise financière*

THE DEVELOPMENT CENTRE

The Development Centre of the Organisation for Economic Co-operation and Development was established by decision of the OECD Council on 23 October 1962 and comprises 23 member countries of the OECD: Austria, Belgium, the Czech Republic, Finland, France, Germany, Greece, Iceland, Ireland, Italy, Korea, Luxembourg, Mexico, the Netherlands, Norway, Poland, Portugal, Slovak Republic, Spain, Sweden, Switzerland, Turkey and the United Kingdom. In addition, the following non-OECD countries are members of the Development Centre: Brazil (since March 1994); Chile (November 1998); India (February 2001); Romania (October 2004); Thailand (March 2005); South Africa (May 2006); Egypt, Israel, and Viet Nam (March 2008); Indonesia (February 2009); Costa Rica, Mauritius, Morocco and Peru (March 2009). The Commission of the European Communities also takes part in the Centre's Governing Board.

The Development Centre, whose membership is open to both OECD and non-OECD countries, occupies a unique place within the OECD and in the international community. Members finance the Centre and serve on its Governing Board, which sets the biennial work programme and oversees its implementation.

The Centre links OECD members with developing and emerging economies and fosters debate and discussion to seek creative policy solutions to emerging global issues and development challenges. Participants in Centre events are invited in their personal capacity.

A small core of staff works with experts and institutions from the OECD and partner countries to fulfil the Centre's work programme. The results are discussed in informal expert and policy dialogue meetings, and are published in a range of high-quality products for the research and policy communities. The Centre's *Study Series* presents in-depth analyses of major development issues. *Policy Briefs* and *Policy Insights* summarise major conclusions for policy makers; *Working Papers* deal with the more technical aspects of the Centre's work.

For an overview of the Centre's activities, please see www.oecd.org/dev.

ISBN: 978-92-64-07551-1 © OECD 2009

Foreword

This publication is part of the Development Centre's Work on Financing Development, which explores responses to the new challenges for bilateral aid arising in the context of the global economic crisis.

ISBN: 978-92-64-07551-1 © OECD 2009

Acknowledgements

Financial support by the Swiss Agency for Development and Cooperation (SDC) is gratefully acknowledged.

The author would like to thank Dilan Ölcer for her research support, and Helmut Reisen for overall guidance. Robert Cornell provided some challenging editing and useful ideas on content. Although his views differ substantially from my own, Professor Paul Hoebink made some very pertinent comments which were taken into account when drafting this study. Felix Zimmermann and Guillaume Grosso provided some very helpful comments on an earlier draft of this paper. A very special thank you goes to Annalisa Prizzon, who provided much valuable feedback, critical input and many helpful suggestions. Any remaining errors remain of course the responsibility of the author.

Table of Contents

ISBN: 978-92-64-07551-1 © OECD 2009

List of Acronyms

AGOA	African Growth and Opportunity Act
CAS	Country Assistance Strategies
CDF	Comprehensive Development Framework
CIESIN	Center for International Earth Science Information Network
CPIA	Country Policy and Institutional Assessment
DAC	Development Assistance Committee
DANIDA	Danish International Development Agency
DFI	Direct Foreign Investment
DFID	Department for International Development
ECLAC	Economic Commission for Latin America and the Caribbean
EBRD	European Bank of Reconstruction and Development
ESAF	Enhanced Structural Adjustment Facility
GPP	Good Practice Principles
GRA	General Resources Account
GSP	Generalised System of Preferences
IBRD	International Bank for Reconstruction and Development
IDA	International Development Association
IFAD	International Fund for Agricultural Development
IFC	International Finance Corporation
IFI	International Financial Institutions
IMF	International Monetary Fund
LDC	Least Developed Country
MCA	Millennium Challenge Account
MDG	Millennium Development Goal
MONA	Monitoring Fund Arrangements
NEPAD	New Economic Partnership for Development
NGO	Non-governmental organisation
PFM	Performance Finance Management
PIU	Project Implementation Unit
PRGF	Poverty Reduction and Growth Facilities
PRSC	Poverty Reduction Support Credit
PRSP	Poverty Reduction Strategy Paper
SAP	Structural Adjustment Programme
SIDA	Swedish International Development Cooperation Agency
SLF	Short-term Liquidity Facility
SWAps	Sector Wide Approaches
WEO	World Economic Outlook
WTO	World Trade Organization

ISBN: 978-92-64-07551-1 © OECD 2009

Preface

Since the Paris Declaration of 2005, there has been a genuine reappraisal of the modality of aid giving. "Good policy environments" and "national ownership" have become key elements within the new framework. Nevertheless, although the lexicon of the donor community has moved on, "aid conditionality" is still very much part and parcel of aid-giving. Where do the controversies persist on aid conditionality? How successful have donors been in stemming the rising tide of conditionality of the 1980s and 1990s? Does the donor community practise what it preaches in terms of aid allocation according to governance and developmental criteria? And what implications does the financial crisis have for the sustainability of existing conditionality frameworks? These are some of the questions that this study attempts to address.

The study reiterates a now commonplace conclusion that policy-based conditionality has been broadly ineffective. But it is a conclusion which merits repetition, as the logical consequence of it has been ignored – the recommendation that most policy-based conditionality should be phased out. The paper also dwells extensively on the shift in recent years away from *ex post* conditionality and towards *ex ante* selectivity. It is argued that while some form of selectivity will inevitably be exercised by donors, the criteria should not be excessively detailed or exhaustive, or donors will risk replacing one form of conditionality with another, and end up marginalising many of the neediest countries.

The study also looks at the implications of different aid modalities for conditionality. Since the 1980s, donor preferences have changed markedly, increasingly favouring programme over project aid. Budget support in particular has been one of the most favoured modalities of delivering aid in recent years. But paradoxically, despite its professed objectives of enhancing recipient ownership of policies, budget support has often inadvertently led to a situation whereby donors try to control the development agenda more extensively than they have in the past. The study suggests that donors should look again at the relative merits of less ambitious forms of programme aid (e.g. SWAps) and project aid.

In addition, given the scale of the current credit crisis and the global imbalances which underlie the international financial system, it would seem apparent that rich countries also require some form of external discipline themselves in making the necessary macroeconomic adjustments. Conditionality, the author argues, "should no longer be a one-way street". The point may be a provocative one, but against the backdrop of the most serious economic crisis in the last 60 years, it is a point which merits serious attention.

Finally, a lot is at stake for the donor community. A number of highly critical studies have recently been published on international aid. The Rwandan government has announced plans about how it intends to end aid dependence. Criticisms of the international aid architecture are thus gaining momentum. Conditionality is one of the major bones of contention between donors and recipients. The crisis has magnified those long-standing grievances. The problem of conditionality needs to be dealt with in a more serious, transparent and even-handed manner than it has in the past. It would be reckless for the donor community to ignore these warning signs.

Javier Santiso
Director, OECD Development Centre
Paris
July 2009

ISBN: 978-92-64-07551-1 © OECD 2009

Chapter 1

Introduction

The international financial crisis, which started in July 2007 but took a decided turn for the worst in September 2008, has given a renewed prominence to the international financial institutions (IFIs), especially the World Bank and the International Monetary Fund (IMF). Before the crisis struck, both institutions had confronted sharply declining demand for their services. Benefiting from extremely favourable external circumstances (particularly high commodity prices), many developing countries no longer had pressing needs for the financial resources of the IFIs. Moreover, because accepting their funds usually implied heavy conditionality, many developing countries preferred other sources of finance.

But the onset of the financial crisis suddenly saw a renewed role for both the World Bank and the IMF. As private sector finance rapidly dried up, the IFIs were required to step in to fill the breach. But because of the sheer gravity of the crisis, there are growing voices calling for the IFIs to relinquish the comprehensive conditionality normally attached to their loans (Wolf, 2008a). Today's exceptional circumstances may indeed spur the re-evaluation of the whole issue of conditionality already under way within the development community. The strong impetus for reform touches on how both the multilaterals and bilateral aid donors disburse their funds. This study explores the underlying issues.

The long-standing debates on aid conditionality (see, *inter alia*, Dreher, 2008, Burnside and Dollar, 2000; Killick, 1998; Mosley *et al.*, 1991; Bird, 1985; Williamson, 1983; Dell, 1981) tie intimately with those over the perceived failure of aid, particularly in sub-Saharan Africa (SSA), to catalyse the kind of development that its proponents had expected. Conscious of the extent of this failure, since the end of the 1990s donors have promoted a *New Aid Agenda*, as articulated in the Paris Declaration of 2005 (OECD, 2005). As a result, the lexicon of the aid industry has shifted away from conditionality and back towards ideas of "ownership" and "partnership". Discussions on "ownership", "reciprocal conditionality" or "development contracts" are not in fact new. The ideas can be traced back at least to the 1980s when promoted by authors such as Stoltenberg (1989) (for a summary, see Polak, 1991).

Arguably, the emphasis on recipient country "ownership" is not merely a question of semantics. A sincere reappraisal of the modality of aid giving has occurred in the last decade, with a notable shift in emphasis towards greater donor alignment and co-ordination. Though hotly disputed, one key element in this new consensus is the importance of *ex post* selectivity – the idea that donors should more actively discriminate among potential recipients, prioritising countries that show evidence of good policy environments and can best articulate national ownership (in the eyes of the donors) (Oya, 2006).

Yet questions remain. Conditionality is in effect the other side of the coin of ownership, for without relinquishing or at least reducing conditionality, ownership is impossible. Which controversies still persist on conditionality? How successfully have donors stemmed its rising tide of the 1980s and 1990s? What does the empirical evidence reveal regarding the impact of conditionality on growth and development? Are donors capable of identifying the "right" set of policies? Does the donor community practise what it preaches in terms of aid allocation according to governance and developmental criteria? If not, then donor countries are sending ambiguous signals to recipients, and even the most carefully designed conditionality is likely to fail. And what implications does the financial crisis have for the sustainability of existing conditionality frameworks?

A lot is at stake in these questions, and not only for the developing country recipients of aid. The conditionality issue has frequently generated tensions and disagreements among donors themselves. One notable example arose in September 2006, when the British government threatened to withhold funds pledged to the World Bank if it did not follow through on an earlier commitment to ease terms on which its aid was given, after concern was raised about the stringent conditionality implicit in the Bank's anticorruption strategy. At the time a number of other European ministers took a similar position to that adopted by the United Kingdom[1].

No consensus yet exists on how to reduce conditionality and enhance ownership (Zimmermann and McDonnell, 2008; Whitfield and Fraser, 2009).Yet ultimately the donor community has priorities other than prolonging a rarefied debate on the nature of ownership and the *optimal* degree of conditionality – in

ISBN: 978-92-64-07551-1 © OECD 2009

particular there is the pressing need to deal with some of the serious structural problems identified in the Paris Declaration, such as aid fragmentation and the lack of co-ordination amongst donors. In this sense, the debates on conditionality detract attention from some reforms which require urgent attention. Indeed, we shall argue that in some senses the whole debate is damaging to the interests of the donor community, as it brings into sharp relief the lack of coherence of the application of their own policies.

Change is being forced on donors in any case. In recent years, new protagonists have brought what might be defined as a "new realism" to donor-recipient relations. China, especially, challenges received wisdom on ownership and conditionality by giving aid on similar terms to those used by Development Assistance Committee (DAC) members and the World Bank in the 1960s and 1970s, namely through project-based aid tied with agreements on trade and aid, with minimal conditionality and no political dimension. This new competition is evidently popular with recipient governments, and the DAC members no longer have a near-monopoly in the provision of aid. These changes in the international aid architecture provide a useful incentive for the IFIs and DAC members to reconsider constructively their positions on conditionality and ownership.

Why Conditionality?

Aid is often considered quite differently from private international finance. But in reality it is not all that different. Donors could, if they so wished, relinquish all conditionality. But rarely do they do so. Almost all lenders – domestic and international, private and public – stipulate conditions on their loans, with the standard and reasonable justification that lenders have an obligation to their depositors or to themselves to ensure that their loans get repaid. Their fear is not an idle one: defaults have occurred periodically ever since international lending began in the Middle Ages. Since the end of the Napoleonic Wars, several cyclical waves of sovereign lending all started with periods of rapid expansion followed by defaults and then sharp declines (Krasner, 1999; Kindleberger and Aliber, 2005). Lending booms occurred in the 1820s (with loans to the newly independent Latin American states), in the 1850s, late 1860s and early 1870s, late 1880s, from 1904 to 1914, the late 1920s, and 1974 to 1982, and defaults or rescheduling have inevitably followed close behind in their wake. Most Latin American countries defaulted during the first part of the 19th century, as did a number of states of the United States in the 1830s and 1840s. In the 20th century, both Germany and Spain defaulted on their loans (Reinhart and Rogoff, 2008; Kindleberger and Aliber, 2005).

The consequences of systematic defaults can spell disaster for international finance, as future sources of external finance may dry up altogether. Putting conditions on loans thus represents a way of trying to reduce the risks for both lenders and the international financial system as a whole and to avoid moral hazard. In fact, both lenders and borrowers can benefit from judicious conditionality, lenders through a reduced risk of default and borrowers (one may hope) through lower interest rates.

Conditionality can also be a particularly useful tool for governments to be able to push through unpopular policy measures or reform packages. When political capacity is weak but governments accept the desirability of reform, external agencies can be "blamed" for requiring governments to adopt unpopular policies. If responsibility for the adverse effects of the reform is not attributed to the government, but to external actors, then opposition has less to attack (Morrissey, 2001: Frey and Eichenberger, 1994).

What motivates conditionality specifically on aid flows? For even the most enlightened donors acting solely in the best interests of recipients the issue can pose dilemmas difficult if not impossible to resolve satisfactorily. The arguments on both sides – those in favour of comprehensive conditions on the use of donor funds and those in favour of maximum leeway for recipients to determine their own policy priorities (ownership) – are complex. First and foremost, donors have a responsibility to ensure that taxpayers' money is spent appropriately, i.e. for development purposes. Ignoring this can have serious consequences, for scandals regarding the misappropriation of resources have the potential to undermine public support for development aid[2]. Thus aid agreements usually allow donors to stop funding given a significant breakdown in public financial management and accountability. This is known as "fiduciary conditionality", and is the least controversial of all the different manifestations of conditionality.

Conditionality is therefore inevitable in some shape or form. The controversy remains over its depth and breadth (in other words, how stringent and numerous the conditions are). Conditionality has grown enormously in scale and scope since the 1980s debt crisis: aid has become conditional on wide-ranging economic, environmental or social policies, such as macroeconomic stabilisation, privatisation or increased investment in health or education. Conditions may also cover political governance and reform. This is something which arguably goes against the very spirit of democratisation and the contemporary empowerment discourse – "conditionality gone mad" in the

ISBN: 978-92-64-07551-1 © OECD 2009

words of Edwards (1999, p. 118). Andrew Mwenda, a Ugandan journalist, puts this case most emphatically:

> "Why hasn't hundreds of billions of dollars of aid transformed the continent? It's because governments listen too much to aid providers and too little to their own citizens. Because the World Bank and the International Monetary Fund give so much money to governments, they find themselves in the odd position of telling national leaders what their people need… from the outside."[3]

Similar views have been expressed by others. Ravi Kanbur (2000, p. 8), an ex-senior member of staff of the World Bank, argues: "In my view, the real cost to Africa of the current aid system is…the fact that it wastes much national energy and political capital in interacting with donors' agencies, and diverts attention from domestic debate and consensus building."

Conditionality ultimately reflects a lack of donor trust or confidence in the capacity or commitment of the recipient country to implement certain types of reform or policies deemed as desirable. Do recipient countries have a right to expect that donor money does not oblige them to do things that they would not have done otherwise? Streeten (1988, p. 107) sees conditionality as redundant whatever the circumstances: "If the policy prescriptions which form the conditions are truly in the interest of the receiving country, why are they not already pursued by the policy makers?". Others would argue that this presupposes that the recipient government always acts in the best interest of its citizens, a supposition clearly not always valid (Polak, 1991; Buiter, 2004; Calderisi, 2007). Such arguments are equally applicable to donors of course – the benevolent donor always acting from principles of pure altruism is a nice fiction, but a fiction none the less.

Constraints on actions are clearly not always a bad thing. If a country suffers under a brutal dictator or the suppression of basic liberties, constraints on action are welcome. The way in which the donor community spoke with one voice in the aftermath of election violence in Kenya in 2007, obliging the two parties to engage in political dialogue, is a good example of how donors can use their power and influence positively. Nevertheless on the whole developing countries tend to be highly suspicious of the inclusion of human rights or civil liberties as part of the "good governance" package; they argue that donor governments or funding agencies may well use such human-rights conditionality as a pretext to deny aid or trade access to any government considered as politically unacceptable. It is, in short, seen as the "thin end of the wedge".

ISBN: 978-92-64-07551-1 © OECD 2009

Those fears are not totally vain ones. International lending, be it concessionary or commercial, has always been used as a powerful instrument of statecraft. Creditors often worry simply about getting their loans serviced, but ever since the Napoleonic Wars (arguably even going back to Roman times) wealthier states have also used international loans to promote their military, economic and ideological objectives. Such objectives have been especially prominent since the latter part of the 20th century, when the "international financial institutions, which have embodied the values of the more advanced capitalist states, have been more concerned with promoting particular domestic changes in borrowing countries than with being repaid" (Krasner, 1999 p. 149).

Some people in the developing world even see human rights or political conditionality as a greater infringement of national sovereignty than economic conditionality (Singer and Raffer, 1996, p. 164). Although conditionality may be consistent with Westphalian principles of international legal sovereignty, it can obviously compromise domestic autonomy (Krasner, 1999). In this sense, the perceived reasonableness of loan conditions often lies in the eyes of beholders. The history of international finance provides numerous examples. For instance, in 1924 the requirements laid down by J.P. Morgan & Co. when it provided a stabilisation loan to the French government irked many French observers. Yet after the crash of 1929, the shoe was on the other foot and French financiers became lenders to Austria and Germany under overtly political conditions. Similarly the conditionality attached to French loans to the United Kingdom in 1931 encountered much criticism amongst the British public. The lenders insisted on implementing the recommendations of the British May Committee to balance the budget and reduce unemployment benefits, despite many misgivings (especially within the British Labour Party) that this would only aggravate the existing problems of recession (Kindleberger and Aliber, 2005 p. 234). In fact, the United Kingdom found itself in a similar position 30 years later because of the inability of the government to deal with its persistent balance-of-payments problems. Between 1961 and 1976 the United Kingdom was subjected to high conditionality lending under the auspices of the IMF *no fewer than three times*. Although the measures adopted were ultimately successful in restoring the macroeconomic balance (Crawford, 1983), the intervention of the Fund was deeply unpopular at the time and indeed contributed to undermining the Labour governments (after the 1976-79 government, the Labour Party was to spend 18 years out of power).

Historically speaking, then, developing countries have not been the only ones to have suffered the consequences of perceived harsh conditionality or to have complained about it being excessively onerous. Pointedly, however, until the IMF intervention in Iceland in October 2008 no developed countries had

ISBN: 978-92-64-07551-1 © OECD 2009

been a client of the IFIs since the 1970s. And because governments probably tend to endorse more stringent conditionality the less the likelihood that they will face conditions themselves, the changing nature of the IFI client base clearly contributed to more stringent conditionality over time. IMF economist Sidney Dell (1981, p. 14-15) noted:

> "... the startling similarity between the views held today by developing country members of the Fund and the views that were being vigorously advocated by the Europeans at a time when they, too, had to face major balance-of-payments pressures of structural character. If the monetary authorities of countries such as France, the Netherlands and the United Kingdom would like to gain a better understanding of the current insistence by developing countries on the need for access to a larger volume of unconditional resources, they have only to look back at their own files and position papers of the early post-war period. What was sauce for the goose in the late 1940s and early 1950s should, perhaps, be sauce for the gander in the 1980s."

The fact that during the current financial crisis developed countries have again become borrowers means that the question of perceived double standards regarding the imposition of conditionality will again come to the fore. More will be said on this later.

Types of Conditionality

Contemporary donor discourse stresses development co-operation as a partnership. Yet in reality nearly all aid conditionality uses negative incentives (sticks) – threats of aid cuts, sanctions of various kinds, military intervention and commercial or diplomatic retaliation – and positive ones (carrots) – promises of more aid, trade concessions, seats at international negotiating tables or protection by foreign troops (Edwards, 1999, p. 114). This is a classic *principal-agent* type problem, to disburse aid in such a manner as to motivate an agent (the recipient) to act in ways that the principal (the donor) wishes (Killick, 1998). Edwards claims that, despite much disagreement on the impact of conditionality, the carrots generally have had more success than the sticks. Although the point is debatable, recalcitrant governments rarely change their behaviour owing to external pressure; indeed, such pressure can intensify their resolve to resist. The literature on the impact of sanctions is highly relevant here. Sanctions applied to Cuba by the United States since the 1960s have been singularly unsuccessful in catalysing regime change. Indeed it might be argued that they have, perversely, strengthened the position of the Cuban government,

ISBN: 978-92-64-07551-1 © OECD 2009

not weakened it. Sanctions applied on Iraq after the first Gulf War similarly had little impact on the Iraqi regime (although by all accounts it had a devastating impact on the Iraqi population). On the other hand, in the case of South Africa, although initially sanctions had little impact on the apartheid government, when the United States started really to apply pressure on the South African government with harsher economic sanctions from the mid-1980s onwards, the apartheid regime was eventually forced to capitulate (Davis and Engerman, 2003; Cortright and Lopez, 2000).

An alternative way of looking at the question distinguishes whether conditionality affects mainly *actions, outcomes* or *processes* (Buiter, 2004). In recent years, *policy* conditionality (action-based conditionality) has been increasingly supplanted by *outcome* conditionality. Through its "MDG Contracts", the European Commission has been especially active in promoting a results-based approach whereby a proportion of its general budget support is conditioned on the rate of progress towards the Millennium Development Goals. Linking conditionality more clearly to improvements in human development indicators has a lot of potential benefits. In practice, however, key outcomes tend to lag far behind actions, making it very difficult to donors to evaluate fairly the performance of the aid recipient. Worse still from the point of view of evaluating performance, the contribution of the particular action demanded by donors to the eventual outcome may be hard to identify, measure and verify. Precisely because of this, conditions should affect only policy instruments genuinely under the recipient government's control and demonstrably linked to the policy targets at which they aim (Mosley, 1987, p. 34). The existence of external shocks (e.g. climatic disasters or a sharp reduction in the price of a country's exports) complicates matters further still – if targets are not met it becomes unclear whether this is due to reasons beyond the control of the recipient government (*force majeure*) or the poor implementation of the agreed policies. Put bluntly, donors often simply do not know enough about whether conditionalities have been satisfied by the recipient governments. Finally, *process conditionality* tries to predetermine the instruments of policy implementation, rather than the policies themselves. In a strict sense, this is governance conditionality, on which more will be said later.

A further important distinction involves the time period and the indicator of performance on which aid is conditional (Collier, 2006, pp. 1487-89). The period can be *ex ante* or *ex post*, i.e. either forward-looking or backward-looking. *Ex ante* policy conditionality has existed for a long time, first put in place formally by the IMF with the 1969 amendment of its Articles of Agreement (Box 1.1). As a modality for conditioning aid, it received a major impetus from the World Bank in the 1980s in the form of Structural Adjustment Programmes (SAPs).

ISBN: 978-92-64-07551-1 © OECD 2009

The World Bank innovated with SAP lending partly because it realised that it often operated in seriously deficient policy environments (giving rise to a whole debate over the "right" environment). SAPs were born as instruments aimed at improving policy through negotiated aid conditionality; aid flowed on the promise of policy reform, an explicit type of *ex ante* conditionality. Critics of such *ex ante* strategies say that donors may use them as excuses to apply conditions which were never viable in the first place. According to Sender (2002), the World Bank has shown itself to be masterful at shifting the blame towards developing countries in this way, arguing that, if only recipient governments had shown sufficient resolve and had "stayed the course", they would have achieved the beneficial results of the reforms. This kind of semantic defence of policy means that it is possible in principle to defend absolutely any reform agenda, no matter how far divorced it is from the realities of the developing country or how poorly designed the policies are.

Box 1.1. **IMF Conditionality**

Preconditions are actions taken by a country before the IMF executive board will authorise a programme.

Performance criteria are benchmarks that, if violated by a country, lead to suspension of further loan disbursements by the Fund until a new agreement is reached.

Policy understandings are actions that a country agrees to take but that do not have any explicit sanction associated with nonperformance.

Typical IMF Financing Preconditions and Performance Criteria

- General commitment to co-operate with the IMF in setting policies
- Reducing government spending, budget deficits, and foreign (external) debt
- Reducing the rate of money growth to control inflation
- Ending government monopolies (i.e. privatisation)
- Deregulating industries and reforming the banking sector
- Redirecting domestic credit from the public to the private sector
- Ending government wage, price, and interest-rate controls and government subsidies
- Raising real interest rates to market levels
- Removing barriers to export growth
- Lowering tariffs, ending quotas, and removing exchange controls and discriminatory exchange rates
- Maintaining adequate levels of international reserves
- Devaluing the currency for countries in "fundamental disequilibrium"

Source: www.imfsite.org/conditionality/whatis.html

ISBN: 978-92-64-07551-1 © OECD 2009

Despite the great upsurge of *ex ante* conditionality in the 1980s and 1990s, a consensus holds that it failed (see *inter alia* Mosley *et al.*, 1991; Dollar and Svensson, 2000; Glennie, 2008). The failure reflected three major weaknesses. First, governments learned to play the system by reneging on their promises. Aid was committed on the basis of promises, yet the limited continuity in World Bank decision taking and strong incentives to disburse made enforcement through future aid commitments not credible (Kanbur, 2000). Indeed, some governments were able to promise the same reform to the Bank several times over. One of the most cited examples of this in the literature was Kenya under President Moi, whose government often promised reforms but subsequently failed to implement[4]. Killick (1998) provides a number of other examples of this type of problem. This weakness straightforwardly illustrates a class of problems known in economics as *time inconsistency* (Collier, 2006). Second, coercive promotion of policy reform sometimes deepened governments' resistance to policy change, such as in the case of Zambia under President Kaunda (although some recipients also used the imposition of reforms to shift blame towards the donor community for policies that they may have endorsed anyway). Third, perhaps fundamentally, the design of the overall policy framework within which the SAPs were applied had flaws, a question to which we will return later.

Frustration with the poor results from old-style SAPs eventually gave way to a new kind of policy based on the principle of *ex post* selectivity, i.e. selecting candidates for aid based on past performance in terms of growth, poverty reduction, human rights, etc. The shift derived principally from the well-known and controversial Burnside-Dollar (2000) finding that aid is effective only where policies are good, yet has no ability to influence those policies (Mosley *et al.*, 2004 p. 218). Collier argues that such *ex post* conditionality provides the strongest incentive effect on recipient governments because the donor specifies precisely both the amount and timing of aid that it will provide and the government performance that is required to obtain it. The best recent example of this kind of conditionality is the US Millennium Challenge Account (MCA, Box 1.2).

ISBN: 978-92-64-07551-1 © OECD 2009

Box 1.2 **The New Aid Architecture and the New Aid Conditionality: The Millennium Challenge Account**

In a speech on 14 March 2002 President Bush directed that countries be identified based on "a set of clear and concrete and objective criteria" that would be applied "rigorously and fairly." The President stated that the Millennium Challenge Account will "reward nations that root out corruption, respect human rights, and adhere to the rule of law... invest in better health care, better schools and broader immunisation... [and] have more open markets and sustainable budget policies, nations where people can start and operate a small business without running the gauntlets of bureaucracy and bribery."

The following 17 indicators (with sources), "chosen because of the relative quality and objectivity of their data", country coverage, public availability, and correlation with growth and poverty reduction, will be used to assess national performance relative to governing justly, investing in people, and encouraging economic freedom.

Governing Justly:
1. Civil Liberties (Freedom House)
2. Political Rights (Freedom House)
3. Voice and Accountability (World Bank Institute)
4. Government Effectiveness (World Bank Institute)
5. Rule of Law (World Bank Institute)
6. Control of Corruption (World Bank Institute)

Investing in People:
7. Immunisation Rates (World Health Organization)
8. Public Expenditure on Health (World Health Organization)
9. Girls' Primary Education Completion Rate (UNESCO)
10. Public Expenditure on Primary Education (UNESCO/national sources)
11. Natural Resource Management (CIESIN/Yale)

Promoting Economic Freedom:
12. Business Start Up (IFC)
13. Inflation (IMF WEO)
14. Trade Policy (Heritage Foundation)
15. Regulatory Quality (World Bank Institute)
16. Fiscal Policy (national sources/IMF WEO)
17. Land Rights and Access (IFAD/IFC)

Source: MCA : http://www.mcc.gov/

ISBN: 978-92-64-07551-1 © OECD 2009

One laudable aspect of the MCA is that it very much puts the developing country in the driving seat, making the recipient responsible for the selection of projects. Nevertheless, such a strategy has obvious risks. Arguably, the MCA's *ex post* selectivity is so sweeping as to make accessing such finance practically very difficult. Although it was set up in 2002 and compacts were signed with developing countries totalling nearly USD 3 billion, the MCA had disbursed only USD 69 million by March 2007 (Kharas, 2008, p. 2). Countries have also had problems complying with conditions for the MCA *ex ante*. In this sense, the MCA does not rigorously fit into the category of *ex post* selectivity. For example, Honduras was the first country in the Americas to sign an agreement for additional aid from the Millennium Challenge Account, with an agreement to spend USD 215 million in Honduras over five years, improving roads and helping farmers. But continued disbursement of this money was subsequently thrown into doubt because American officials have judged Honduras to have made insufficient effort to eliminate corruption in Central America[5].

In general, then, strategies of *ex post* conditionality run into some very difficult practical problems. Particularly in Africa, which has the majority of poor countries but not many governments that yet practise "good" policies in the World Bank sense, the logic of selectivity leads donors to an undesirable situation: donor aid administrations feel forced to choose between under-spending their budgets (and thus losing influence both with their developing-country partners and within their own governments) and giving aid to bad-policy countries (Mosley *et al.*, 2004, p. 218). Table 1.1 reveals the implications of a pure selectivity strategy. Using the calculated poverty-reduction elasticities, a donor pursuing such a strategy based on the efficiency of poverty reduction would end up dedicating its funding to just two regions – East Asia and Pacific and South Asia. But the counterpart of identifying "aid darlings" on past performance is the possibility of also of creating "aid orphans". The poorest countries in sub-Saharan Africa would be excluded from its list of beneficiaries. This makes the selectivity approach difficult to defend as a general philosophy for allocating development aid. As Schmitz (2006, p. 6) notes,

> "development policy committed to reducing poverty on a global scale cannot treat recipients differently without losing credibility ... it is clear that a selectivity strategy is not an option for the majority of donors .... First, it would require defining adequate general, yet at the same time tailor-made, criteria for political and institutional framework conditions that are conducive to economic growth. *This is obviously beyond the donor's prognostic capabilities.* Second, the donors would have to select recipients particularly worthy of

ISBN: 978-92-64-07551-1 © OECD 2009

support based on these criteria. And third, this decision would have to be consistently implemented, that is to say, without the influence of special interests. A strategy of selectivity thus places demands on the coherence and convergence of donors' interests and objectives that they cannot meet."

Table 1.1. **Aid, Growth and Poverty Reduction by Region**

Regions	(1) Poverty Reduction 1990-99 (percentage points/year)	(2) Growth GDP % 1990-99 (percentage points/year)	(3) = (1)/(2) Poverty reduction per unit of growth	(4) ODA/GNP (%), 1992	(5) = (1)/(4) Poverty reduction per unit of aid
East Asia and Pacific	1.05	7.18	0.15	0.34	3.09
Middle East/North Africa	0.23	0.66	0.35	1.23	0.19
Latin America/ Caribbean	0.23	1.23	0.19	0.30	0.77
East Europe/Central Asia	-0.68	0.13	-5.23	2.17	-0.31
South Asia	2.50	3.33	0.75	0.66	3.77
Developing World	0.92	3.81	0.24	1.45	0.63

Note: Calculations are based on annualised reductions in country poverty headcount percentages (using as the poverty line either USD 1/day or a national one, depending on data availability) using population shares as weights.
Source: Mosley *et al.* (2004, p. 222).

StatLink ⏰ http://dx.doi.org/10.1787/704038540655

To summarise the discussion so far, Table 1.2 illustrates the basic positions on the type of conditionality. A cleavage has gradually emerged between those that favour outcome-based conditionality, and those that favour a policy-based approach. The EU is the body which has probably gone furthest down the road of pursuing outcome-based conditionality. In 2005 the European Commission published *EC Budget Support: An Innovative Approach to Conditionality* (European Commission, 2005) which defines outcome-based conditionality as aid disbursed against "progress attained for a number of indicators, mainly of results in the reduction of aspects of poverty directly linked to service delivery and of public financial management". Thus social indicators such as the percentage of children vaccinated or the percentage of primary school enrolment are now expressly identified. Eurodad (2008) questions whether the EC's change in practice has been as bold as the theoretical approach, but the shift towards creating greater incentives through conditionality for poverty reduction is clearly to be welcomed.

Table 1.2. **The Matrix of Design Options for Conditionality**

	Policies	Outcomes	Governance
Ex ante	World Bank in the 1980s; IMF	European Union	
Ex post	World Bank (IDA); DFID		United States (MCA)

Source: Collier (2006).

In fact, only one major player, the IMF, now maintains explicit *ex ante* conditionality, and even the Fund is shifting its position in the light of the financial crisis. The Fund has also taken note of the ownership issue by attempting to rein back the scope of its conditionality to policy changes demonstrably critical to the success of programme. As we shall see later, the evidence on whether the Fund has achieved this objective is ambiguous. Meanwhile, the World Bank has gradually shifted from *ex ante* to *ex post* policy conditionality, allocating aid based on attained levels of policy reform rather than on promises of policy change.

The unifying instrument for World Bank conditionality has been the Poverty Reduction Strategy Paper (PRSP), a controversial and complicated mechanism introduced in 1999 that purportedly puts recipient countries in charge of defining overarching strategies for poverty reduction and growth. PRSPs were intended to be "country-driven and owned, based on broad-based participatory processes for formulation, implementation, and outcome-based monitoring" (IMF and World Bank, 2001: Annex 2). Nevertheless, because PRSPs also constitute the sole basis for debt relief and new concessional lending from the Bretton Woods institutions, they inevitably skew power in the partnership strongly in favour of the creditor (Browne, 2007, p. 55). This is not the place to enter into a detailed critique of the evidence regarding PRSPs (some more will be said on this subject in the following section)[7]. But it is revealing that PRSPs fail to differ substantially from one another, detracting from their credibility as documents which truly reflect a process of democratic consultation (Stewart and Wang, 2003). Moreover, because they are subject to the approval of both the IMF and World Bank boards, in an important sense PRSPs have expanded the scope of conditionality.

ISBN: 978-92-64-07551-1 © OECD 2009

Notes

1. See "Minister 'Invented' World Bank Row" by Krishna Guha and Alan Beattie, FT.com site. Published: 19 September 2006.

2. The concern is a legitimate one. Nevertheless, it is worth noting that surveys of public opinion show support to be surprisingly resilient to aid "failure" – that is to say, there is a significant group of people who would appear to be supportive of aid even when they know, or believe, that it has not been working well (Riddell, 2007, pp. 115-116; OECD, 2005).

3. Cited at www.ethanzuckerman.com/blog/2007/06/04/getting-rowdy-with-andrew-mwenda/ (accessed 24 February 2008).

4. Wrong (2009) provides an informative account of relations between donors and Kenyan governments since independence.

5. See *The Economist* 30 October 2008, "Zelaya plays the Chávez card", www.economist.com/world/americas/displaystory.cfm?story_id=12522958

6. A good recent review of the evidence can be found in Riddell (2007, Chapter 13).

ISBN: 978-92-64-07551-1 © OECD 2009

Chapter 2

Shifting Aid Modalities: A Brief Historical Recapitulation

Conditionality has grown over the last three decades in a way probably unimaginable in the early years of development aid. Donors now have an enormous influence on policy decision making and execution in areas as disparate as democracy, judicial reform, corporate governance, health, education and environmental policy (Chang, 2005). As Robert Chambers (2005, p. 39) has noted,

> "Now, to a degree that during the 1960s would have been vilified as gross neo-colonialism, in many small and low-income countries – especially in sub-Saharan Africa – lenders and donors not only fund much government expenditure (over 50 per cent in Uganda, for example), but also call many of the policy shots."

A little historical perspective on the way in which conditionality has evolved is thus important to put these shifts in context, for it ties intimately with the way in which aid disbursement has changed. At the risk of excessive simplification, one can distinguish broadly between five different periods in donor-recipient relations:

The Post War Period 1947-1960. In the first post-war decade, conditionality was far less obtrusive than it became after 1980. One reason for this was that the industrial countries themselves were still major clients of the IFIs – they had decisive influence and control and were reluctant to countenance excessively intrusive conditionality. The Marshall Plan did carry some conditions, but on the whole conditionality as we now understand it was limited to IMF lending. Even here, the original remit of the IMF was specifically to mitigate balance-of-payments crises and initially no specific provision was made for conditionality.

ISBN: 978-92-64-07551-1 © OECD 2009

In 1950 the Fund's Executive Directors accepted a mild form of conditionality in order to persuade the United States to continue financing its operations. The 1950 decision recognised that members could only draw from their gold tranches (the first 25 per cent of their quotas) without restrictions. But not until 1969 were the Articles of Agreement formally amended to provide for conditionality above the first credit tranche. As Krasner (1999, p. 146) puts it, "the Americans ultimately prevailed [in their view of imposing harsher conditionality] because they had the money." With regard to the World Bank, despite the frequent claim that its loans had no conditionality until the 1980s, the Bank held back its very first loan of USD 250 million to France in 1947 until the French government gave evidence of its economic soundness by the expulsion of Communists from the cabinet (Caulfield, 1996, p. 53). In the 1950s, the World Bank attempted to condition its lending on countries' establishing some form of overall economic planning (Hirschman, 1987, p. 184)[1].

The Development Optimism of the 1960s and 1970s. In the 1960s and 1970s, aid towards developing countries was focused on projects in infrastructure and agriculture. The McNamara years at the World Bank saw rapid expansion in all donors' funding, but with low or even non-existent conditionality attached. Project aid became established across all sectors in the portfolios of most donors. And on the whole the returns on those portfolios were perfectly respectable (Mosley and Eeckhout, 2000, p. 134). As the 1970s progressed, developing countries also obtained large-scale loans, principally from private banks, on the back of high commodity prices and strong growth performance, as the financial system recycled the excess liquidity stemming from petrol-dollar balances accruing in producer nations. The banks generally considered sovereign lending safest, and conditions on loans were lax. The Cold War, too, created an additional spur to financing, as the IFIs willingly provided development finance to governments with strong anti-communist credentials (e.g. Zaire [now the Democratic Republic of Congo], Indonesia, Chile, etc.). As the international economic context changed, however, with a sharp rise in interest rates when the United States and the United Kingdom adopted monetarist policies, profligacy gave way to austerity. This hit developing countries particularly hard as commodity prices collapsed, and many ran into difficulties in meeting payments on loans.

The 1980s Debt Crisis and Structural Adjustment. The subsequent debt crisis in the early 1980s belatedly alerted the financial community to the fact that sovereign loans were not nearly as safe as the private banking system had supposed and ushered in a new set of donor-recipient relations. This gave ample space for new activism among the IFIs. Buira (2003, p. 73) argues that this moment decisively accounted for the rise in conditionality and resulted in large

ISBN: 978-92-64-07551-1 © OECD 2009

part from the US Treasury's influence on the IMF, reflecting the new priorities of the intellectual revolution under Thatcher and Reagan that supported the shift towards monetarism. In 1985, US Treasury Secretary James Baker called on the World Bank and the IMF to help liberalise market institutions and strengthen the private sector. The IMF supported the Baker initiative, which included provisions for structural conditionality and stronger collaboration between the IMF and the Bank. In the aftermath of the debt crisis, project loans – however big, however fast – did not suffice (Caulfield, 1996; Singer and Raffer, 1996; Collier, 2006). The need for urgent action to guarantee the solvency of the international financial system led to the rapid development of programme aid. Taking the DAC definition (OECD, 1991, p. 5), "programme assistance consists of all contributions made available to a recipient country for general development purposes, i.e. balance-of-payments support, general budget support and commodity assistance, not linked to specific project activities." Under the expansion of programme aid (especially SAPs), conditionality expanded in a way previously inconceivable. The IFIs started to require whole sets of conditions for financing eligibility, and many cash-strapped developing countries felt incapable of resisting. The World Bank and the IMF initially limited their conditions principally to budget deficits, monetary expansion, privatisation and trade liberalisation, but this was soon to change.

Mission Creep and Growing Disillusion in the 1990s. The remit of the IFIs then underwent such constant mission creep that, by the time of the 1997 financial crisis, the IMF was actually ordering the Korean government to give independence to the country's central bank and even told private Korean companies how much debt they could take on (Feldstein, 1998; Chang, 2005). The IMF even became involved in areas like environmental policy, about as far from its original remit as could be (Easterly, 2007). One of the reasons for the sharp increase in conditionality over this period was the end of the Cold War. As Lancaster (2007, p. 52-3) notes, diplomatic, commercial, and cultural purposes of aid-giving during the decades preceding the end of the Cold War made policies of selectivity and conditionality difficult. With the end of the Cold War, this constraint was removed. The neoliberal emphasis in US policy towards the IFIs started during the Reagan years continued under the Clinton administration. The Treasury Secretary at the time, Robert E. Rubin, pressured the IMF to amend the Articles of Agreement so that it could require borrowing governments to remove capital controls. The World Bank, too, innovated to expand its remit enormously. Under the leadership of James D. Wolfensohn, it launched a torrent of initiatives like the Strategic Compact, the Partnership Initiative, the Knowledge Bank and the Comprehensive Development Framework (CDF) (Rich, 2002). Pincus and Winters (2002, p. 3) comment that it would be difficult "to think of an issue or constituency that does not in some way fall under the "long-term, holistic approach to development" envisioned by the CDF." Nevertheless, the donor community and IFIs should not by any means bear the whole responsibility for the secular increase in conditionality. In the search for the evasive "holy grail" of development – the "right set of policies" – academic and NGO critics constantly prodded and cajoled the IFIs and donors to widen their remits, accusing them of adopting an excessively narrow, simplified view of the development process. In all this expansion of the IFIs, it did not help that much of the conditionality was negotiated in secret – the IMF's famous Letters of Intent being the most well-known example – creating the impression of unaccountability and a lack of transparency. One result of this enlargement of conditionality was that compliance with IMF programmes in the 1990s was much lower than in the 1970s and 1980s, an outcome that reduced the catalytic effect of such programmes in raising private finance (Toye and Toye, 2004, p. 281). The imposition of cross-conditionality compounded these problems, as access to one agency's finance became conditional upon compliance with the stipulations of a second agency. For instance, the World Bank required (informally) that to be eligible for a structural adjustment credit a country needed also to be in compliance with its IMF programme (Killick, 1998, p. 9). Moreover, many bilateral donors effectively piggy-backed on IFI conditionality; countries such as the United Kingdom, the United States, Germany and the Netherlands made their own aid conditional on previous agreements with the World Bank and the IMF. In other words, the impact of conditionality increasingly went beyond the nominal stipulations in the agreements signed with a particular agency. In the second half of the 1990s, however, the IFIs and the wider donor community became increasingly dispirited with the lack of tangible results from the SAPs and their offshoots, especially the dismal performance of sub-Saharan Africa, which had experienced negligible and even negative rates of per capita income growth since the early 1980s. Countries in other continents which had also undergone structural adjustment also disappointed in terms of resumed economic growth and development. One notable example is Bolivia, which suffered practically stagnant income growth in the 20 years after it first initiated its structural adjustment programme in 1986. Exhaustive evaluations in the 1990s (e.g. Mosley *et al.*, 1991; Killick, 1998) generally confirmed the disappointing performance, although they suffered from methodological limitations and often arrived at nuanced conclusions. Many critics also decried the lack of transparency in the application of conditionality. By 2001, World Bank researchers themselves declared that "conditionality as an instrument to promote reform has been a failure" (Devarajan *et al.*, 2001). The authors subsequently placed caveats on this evaluation, claiming that countries with the desire to reform did indeed achieve

ISBN: 978-92-64-07551-1 © OECD 2009

some results. Yet the overall impression revealed a kind of *policy fatalism*: only countries adopting the right policies would succeed and nothing could be done to persuade or cajole others to change track.

2000 Onwards: The New Aid Agenda. So began a new era in the tortuous history of donor-recipient relations. An OECD paper published in 1996 (OECD, 1996) had already given indications of shifting ground within the donor community. The true catalyst of change, however, probably came with the policy shift of the IFIs from 2000 onwards. Spearheaded by the aforementioned Burnside-Dollar (2000) paper, a new philosophy of aid giving was embraced: only countries adopting "good policies" used aid effectively. Thus it advocates a marked shift towards *ex ante* rather than *ex post* conditionality. The *New Aid Agenda* has many components, but a central one involves broadened and expanded conditionality, a sort of "enhanced Washington Consensus" (Rodrik, 2006), characterised by a combination of economic and political benchmarks and a strong focus on governance and institutional issues (Oya, 2006, p. 6). Drawn up after protracted negotiations between donors, recipient governments and other stakeholders (various representatives of civil society), PRSPs and recipient country "ownership" became central to this new orthodoxy of the donor community. Yet ironically PRSP conditionality has arguably had a much wider impact than traditional contract conditionality because it ties support to policies that change the structures of entire sectors, e.g. the privatisation or liberalisation of electricity systems rather than just one specific contract, such as building a power station. The World Bank's Country Assistance Strategies (CASs) function in much the same way, as a core set of policy conditions to which other World Bank aid is linked (Hall and de la Motte, 2004, p. 4). At the same time, Structural Adjustment Loans gradually morphed into "Poverty Reduction and Growth Facilities" (PRGF), and have remained subject to pervasive conditionality. Concomitantly, the last ten years have seen a more determined push in favour of programme assistance, budget support and global funds. The Paris Declaration (OECD, 2005) set the target for 2010 that 66 per cent of aid flows should be provided in the context of programme-based approaches from a baseline of 43 per cent in 2005. Already, the Netherlands channels approximately 70 per cent of its development assistance through sectoral and general budget support. DFID (UK) disburses approximately 50 per cent of its development assistance through budget support and approximately 25 per cent through Sector Wide Approaches (SWAps). As of June 2006, the World Bank provided approximately 40 per cent of its new lending through budget support (Bissio, 2008, p. 131).

Notes

1. In fact, the industrial countries received loans from the World Bank for only a short period after World War II. Industrial countries were, however, potential IMF borrowers right up until the 1980s. This might explain in part why World Bank conditions in the 1980s were much more numerous than those of the Fund. From then on, the developing countries became the main clients of both institutions, and conditionality became correspondingly more onerous.

ISBN: 978-92-64-07551-1 © OECD 2009

Chapter 3

Is Conditionality Increasing or Diminishing?

The implications of this last big shift in donors' conditionality policies are controversial, and will be examined in more depth later in Chapter 7 of this study. In principle, however, the donor community is now strongly committed to reducing conditionality and enhancing ownership. For instance, the Commission for Africa (2005, p. 314) proclaimed that "policy conditionality...is both an infringement on sovereignty and ineffective." The same year the United Kingdom produced an important policy document boldly committing the government to eliminate it and to adopt a non-interventionist approach: "The United Kingdom will not make our aid conditional on specific policy decisions by partner governments or attempt to impose policy choices on them (including in sensitive economic areas such as privatisation or trade liberalisation)" (DFID, 2005, p. 10). At their July 2005 meeting at Gleneagles, the G-8 leaders confirmed the need for recipient countries to "decide, plan and sequence their economic policies to fit with their own economic strategies for which they should be accountable to their people". Such declarations have been become increasingly frequent since the second half of the 1990s, when disillusions with the results of Structural Adjustment became more widespread. Some countries such as Canada abandoned conditionality altogether. Over the last ten years, then, calls for the reduction of conditionality and enhanced ownership have gained momentum. But how much has really been achieved?

Before answering this question, it is important to recognise that there is a definitional problem. Dreher (2008, p. 4-5) notes that existing definitions of ownership vary widely. Two competing, and potentially contradictory, concepts coexist: ownership as commitment to policies, however they were arrived at; and ownership as control over the process and outcome of choosing policies (Whitfield and Fraser, 2009). Some authors (e.g. Morrissey and Verschoor, 2004, cited in Dreher, *op. cit.*) argue that policies are "owned" if they originate from borrowing country policy makers. Others see ownership in terms of the degree of commitment shown by the recipient country to donor policies! Drazen and Isard (2004) relate ownership not only to the willingness to carry out a programme but also to the technical capacity and political will to implement it.

Leaving aside the complicated question about exactly what "ownership" really means at face value, it is relatively easy to trace trends in terms of the application of conditionality. According to the World Bank's own figures (cited by Riddell, 2007, p. 237), in the early 1980s on average the Bank applied five conditions to their loans and used the same number of benchmarks against which to assess performance. By the end of the decade, the average number of conditions had risen to over 30; they peaked at 45 by 1993, and by 2000 still numbered about 25. The average number of benchmarks trebled in the 1980s and averaged well over ten for the decade of the 1990s. By the mid-1990s, almost 120 countries had some form of adjustment programme. Since then, both IDA and IBRD operations have produced a sharp fall in the number of conditions applied, from around the 20 reported in 2000 to between 10 and 12 in 2007 (Figure 3.1).

Figure 3.1. **Average Number of Conditions in World Bank Lending**

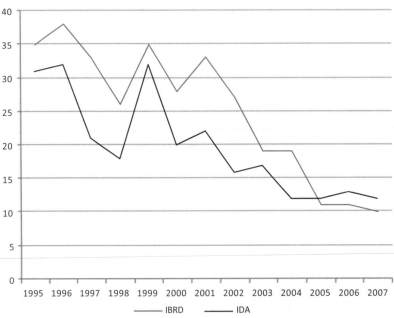

Source: World Bank (2007, p. 5).

StatLink 🔗 http://dx.doi.org/10.1787/703855243571

ISBN: 978-92-64-07551-1 © OECD 2009

The World Bank has made much of this apparent reduction in the overall number of conditions attached to its finance. It has made efforts to curtail the use of conditionality in several sectors – trade and economic management, environment, rural and urban development, and financial and private sector development – but has increased it in the social sectors and public sector governance (Figure 3.2). These shifts can be explained in a number of ways. As more poor developing countries have become members of the World Trade Organization (WTO), trade policy conditionality has in any case become redundant, as trade policy is now constrained by WTO rules. So these trends do not *a priori* suppose less conditionality. The shift towards greater conditionality in the public sector governance sector, including public financial management reform and improvements in financial accountability and budget processes, might seem coherent with the importance placed on the "good governance" paradigm, but is also perhaps the product of greater pressure to privatise public sector services (Hall and de la Motte, 2004).

Figure 3.2. **Thematic Coverage of Conditionality in Policy-Based Lending**

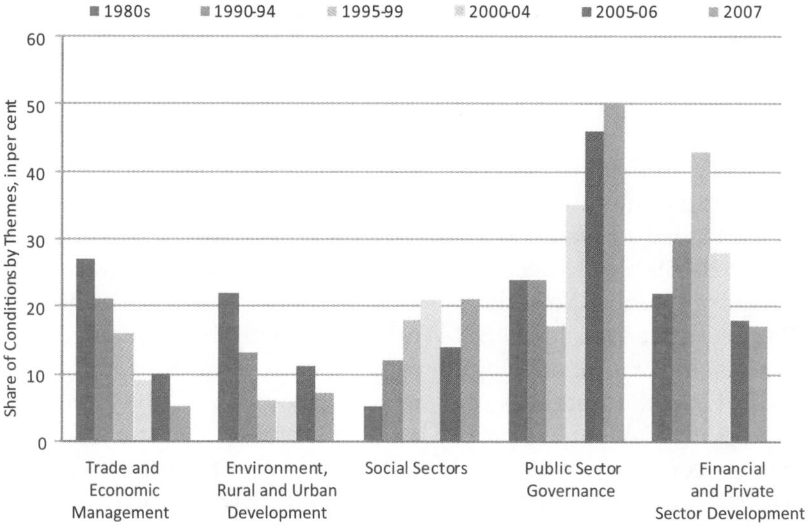

Source: World Bank (2007, p. 6).

StatLink http://dx.doi.org/10.1787/703855647230

Nevertheless, even these figures are controversial. Putting precise numbers on something as qualitative as conditionality is inherently problematic. Eurodad (2007) disputes the World Bank's claim of having reduced conditionality and argues that the fall in the number of conditions stems largely from a drop in the number of non-binding conditions, from 33 per loan before the adoption of Good Practice Principles (GPP) to 24 in 2007. But legally binding conditions have remained unchanged at 13 per loan (Table 3.1). The World Bank makes an important distinction here between "prior actions" – reforms that a government must put in place before it will receive finance – and "benchmarks", which the World Bank considers desirable but non-binding. A World Bank survey in 2005 conceded that policy makers often regarded all these conditions as requirements to obtain development finance[1]. The number of benchmarks has increased as binding conditions have fallen suggesting that part of the reduction in the number of conditions simply resulted from changing their name to benchmarks[2].

Table 3.1. **Average Number of Conditions per World Bank Loan, 2005-07**

	Pre-GPP (average, 09/2003 - 09/2005)	Post-GPP (average, 10/2005 - 06/2007)
Average number of binding conditions	13	13
Average number of non-binding conditions	33	24
Total number of conditions	46	37

Source: Eurodad (2007, p. 9).

StatLink ⬛📊 http://dx.doi.org/10.1787/704128685647

According to Eurodad (2007), even these figures may mislead, as there has been an apparent "bundling" of conditions. For instance, the number of conditions attached to loans for Uganda (one of the countries with the most conditions in 2005) sharply decreased in 2006, partly by counting several policy reforms required by the World Bank as single conditions. Eurodad found that almost 7 per cent of a sample of 1 341 World Bank conditions contained multiple policy actions. Individual developing countries also show an apparently very large disparity in the numbers of conditions they face. Only three of some 60 countries with IDA loans approved between October 2005 and July 2007 had fewer than ten conditions. One was Mozambique, where the donor community had made concerted efforts to reduce conditionality. Rwanda, in contrast, faced 144 conditions in its last Poverty Reduction Support Grant approved at the end of 2006. Senegal faced as many as 99 conditions per loan.

What about IMF conditionality? The facility for low-income countries, the Poverty Reduction and Growth Facility, shows some reduction of conditions prior to the 2004 Guidelines, whereas conditions on the *General Resources Account* (GRA) (which handles by far the largest share of transactions between

ISBN: 978-92-64-07551-1 © OECD 2009

the IMF and its membership) actually increased over the ten years from 1995 to 2004 (Figure 3.3). Moreover, it does not take into account the extent to which conditionality expanded so vigorously in the late 1980s and early 1990s (Figure 3.4). Such a sharp prior increase in conditions makes the subsequent tailing off look less impressive. As the IMF's own internal audit office has conceded:

> "The streamlining initiative did not reduce the volume of conditionality, partly because structural conditions continued to be used to monitor other initiatives such as donors' support programmes and the European Union (EU) accession process. But it helped to shift the composition of conditionality toward IMF core areas and new areas of basic fiduciary reform. At the same time, the IMF moved away from controversial areas where it had little impact and that largely fall within the World Bank's areas of expertise. Nonetheless, Fund arrangements still included conditions that seem not to have been critical to programme objectives." (IMF, 2007, p. 4).

Figure 3.3. **Average Number of IMF Structural Conditions per Programme Year, 1995-2004**

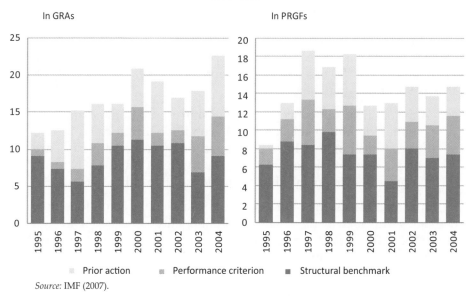

Prior action   Performance criterion   Structural benchmark

Source: IMF (2007).

StatLink http://dx.doi.org/10.1787/704028133725

Figure 3.4. **Average Number of IMF Structural Conditions per Programme Year, 1987-95**

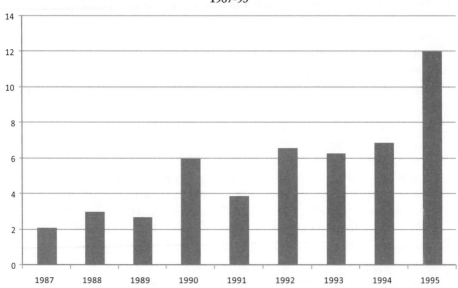

Source: IMF sources, cited in Buira (2003, p. 7).

StatLink ᐧᐧᐧᐧ http://dx.doi.org/10.1787/704032147388

Whether the shift towards new aid delivery modalities (particularly budget support) has helped or hindered progress is also open to debate (and something which is discussed in greater depth in Chapter 7 of this study). Killick (2005, p. 95) argues that:

"A major subject of concern with the shift to programme aid is its potential for adding substantially to conditionality. It could be that the relationships that have developed on a partnership basis are evolving as a substitute for conditionality, but it could easily result in more old-style policy stipulations. It could go either way."

In some dimensions of aid policy, it is clear that conditionality is still onerous, as witnessed by the extensive conditionality associated with initiatives like the MCA (Box 1.2). In any case, donors still place many constraints on host-government policy execution and broader political governance, both through IFI and bilateral conditionalities. The example of Ethiopia (Box 3.1) illustrates the scale of the challenge.

ISBN: 978-92-64-07551-1 © OECD 2009

Box 3.1. **IMF Conditionality in Ethiopia**

According to a study reported by ActionAid (2005, p. 2), the Poverty Reduction Strategy for Ethiopia has over 200 criteria in the matrix which guides disbursement decisions. Recent efforts by budget-support donors to reduce the matrix to 50 criteria have so far floundered. The World Bank alone has upwards of 80 binding and non-binding criteria, encompassing liberalisation of the external sector and interest rates; the reorientation of spending to poverty alleviation; and speedier tax reform, privatisation and the strengthening of the private sector, including removing barriers to foreign bank entry (Afrodad, 2006). Easterly (2007, pp. 210-212) provides an overview of how the IMF still determines the policy environment in Ethiopia. The country was facing lower tax revenues and external loans as well as a major drought. The IMF's "Fifth Review Under the Three Year Arrangement with the Poverty Reduction and Growth Facility" urged the Finance Minister to cut government spending while protecting "poverty-targeted" expenditure. While "the staff welcomes the food security programme" designed by the government in reaction to the drought, the Fund warns the government to be careful that food-security spending not endanger "macroeconomic stability". Easterly goes on to detail other constraints on the Ethiopian Finance Minister's scope of action:

> "The IMF specifies mandatory targets for Ethiopia for international foreign exchange reserves, for the net domestic credit of the central bank, for domestic financing of the government deficit, for government arrears on paying its bills, and for government external borrowing. Other agreements with the IMF include reforming the tax system (including computerisation of the taxpayer identification number and the introduction of the value-added tax); limiting defence spending; limiting the government wage bill, consolidating regional and federal budgets and extra-budgetary accounts, reconciling fiscal and monetary account statistics, letting the market determine the exchange rate, provisioning by commercial banks for overdue loan repayments, privatising the Commercial and Business Bank (CBB), restructuring the Development Bank of Ethiopia (NBE), increasing the autonomy of the NBE; reforming the Commercial Bank of Ethiopia (CBE) based on an audit by the international firm KPMG and a detailed plan agreed upon with the IMF that specifies numerical performance targets, limits any delinquent loan from CBE to two renewals, and transfers co-financed loans from the CBE to the DBE; liberalising trade as a preliminary step in the Integrated Framework for Trade Development in the least-developed countries; rewriting the investment code to limit the role of government to electricity transmission, the postal service and the national airline; tracking debt-relief resources so that they are used for poverty reduction; and improving the compilation of statistics on the balance of payments, monetary indicators, international reserves, and agricultural and industrial production. The government should do all this while consulting with the poor, civil society, nongovernmental organisations, private individuals and the foreign donors on what it should do to reduce poverty, in the context of the Annual Progress Report (APR) on the PRSP."

Finally, as mentioned earlier (see p. 35), conditionality is not limited to aid flows; other policies towards the developing world also impose extensive conditionality. Trade policy provides one example, with the multitude of conditions that apply for preferential market access schemes like the US African Growth and Opportunity Act (AGOA) or the EU's new Generalised System of Preferences (GSP)+ programme (Box 3.2). Conditionality needs consideration in this wider sense – i.e. not only through the prism of aid policies, but also across a range of development-related policies.

Box 3.2. **The EU's New Trade Preferences for Poor Countries: Qualifying for the GSP+**

Trade policy has been given much emphasis in recent years as a complementary instrument to aid as a tool for development. But it is similarly subject to extensive conditionalities. In June 2005, the European Union announced a new framework for its long-standing Generalised System of Preferences (GSP) for developing countries, in force since 1971. It covers a broader range of products and offers preferences substantially improved over the standard GSP and comparable to those available to other "most preferred" states. To benefit from these additional preferences, a country must have ratified and be effectively implementing all core human and labour rights in UN/ILO conventions and at least seven (of 11) conventions related to environment and governance principles.

Core Human and Labour Rights in UN/ILO Conventions

1. International Covenant on Civil and Political Rights
2. International Covenant on Economic, Social and Cultural Rights
3. International Convention on the Elimination of All Forms of Racial Discrimination
4. Convention on the Elimination of All Forms of Discrimination Against Women
5. Convention Against Torture and other Cruel, Inhuman or Degrading Treatment or Punishment
6. Convention on the Rights of the Child
7. Convention on the Prevention and Punishment of the Crime of Genocide
8. Convention concerning Minimum Age for Admission to Employment
9. Convention concerning the Prohibition and Immediate Action for the Elimination of the Worst Forms of Child Labour
10. Convention concerning the Abolition of Forced Labour
11. Convention concerning Forced or Compulsory Labour
12. Convention concerning Equal Remuneration of Men and Women Workers for Work of Equal Value
13. Convention concerning Discrimination in Respect of Employment and Occupation

---

ISBN: 978-92-64-07551-1 © OECD 2009

14. Convention concerning Freedom of Association and Protection of the Right to Organise
15. Convention concerning the Application of the Principles of the Right to Organise and to Bargain Collectively
16. International Convention on the Suppression and Punishment of the Crime of Apartheid.

Conventions Related to the Environment and Good Governance

17. Montreal Protocol on Substances that Deplete the Ozone Layer
18. Basel Convention on the Control of Trans-boundary Movements of Hazardous Wastes and Their Disposal
19. Stockholm Convention on Persistent Organic Pollutants
20. Convention on International Trade in Endangered Species of Wild Fauna and Flora
21. Convention on Biological Diversity
22. Cartagena Protocol on Bio-safety
23. Kyoto Protocol to the United Nations Framework Convention on Climate Change
24. United Nations Single Convention on Narcotic Drugs (1961)
25. United Nations Convention on Psychotropic Substances (1971)
26. United Nations Convention against Illicit Traffic in Narcotic Drugs and Psychotropic Substances (1988)
27. United Nations Convention against Corruption (Mexico)

Notes

1. As Eurodad (2007, p. 9) puts it, "Benchmarks are regarded as potential future prior actions or legal conditions or important to maintain a good relationship with the Bank. Whilst we recognise these are not as punitive as formal conditions, benchmarks are still used to direct countries down reform paths that may be inappropriate and are thus a major cause of concern for NGOs".

2. I am grateful to my colleague Helmut Reisen for pointing this out to me.

ISBN: 978-92-64-07551-1 © OECD 2009

Chapter 4

A Brief Review of Some Empirical Studies
of Conditionality's Impact

Much, though not all, of the empirical literature on the impact on conditionality covers IMF programmes, for straightforward reasons: the conditionality associated with these programmes is the most long-standing, and data are more readily available. Since the 1990s, the IMF itself has provided data on compliance with its programme conditionality, through its database on Monitoring Fund Arrangements (MONA)[1]. The empirical studies on the impact of conditionality have two different strands. A large literature admirably summarised by Dreher (2008) tries to determine the extent to which recipients have complied with conditionality. This literature generally concludes that compliance is lax (see, *inter alia*, Mecagni, 1999 and Edwards, 2001). The second strand looks at the impacts of compliance on economic policy and outcomes.

The empirical literature conveys an inevitably mixed message, given the different methodologies, samples and approaches used. But the overriding impression is that conditionality has largely been ineffective in enhancing the impact of development aid on growth or human development. One of the first papers to influence the debate was Mosley *et al.* (1991), which noted that compliance with World Bank policy conditions had only a weak impact on GDP growth rates. However, the estimation techniques used for the cross-country regressions had some severe limitations (McGillivray and Morrissey, 1999). As noted in Chapter 2, the seminal paper of Burnside and Dollar (2000) (an earlier version of which had served as an input to the World Bank's influential *Assessing Aid* document published in 1998) started the controversy over *ex ante* conditionality, declaring that aid has, on average, little impact on growth but a more positive impact in a good policy environment. They concluded that aid should be allocated according to a more selective approach, making it conditional on the existing policy environment.

This finding has received criticism ever since it was published (e.g. McGillivray *et al.*, 2006, Deaton *et al.* 2006)[2]. Hansen and Tarp (2001) produced one of the first direct rebuttals, finding that aid is not conditional on the adoption of good policies. Noorbakhsh and Paloni (2001) do find that compliance with conditionality can raise growth rates, but make the important distinction between strong, average and weak compliers. They see little difference in growth performance between the strong and weak ones. They also note that in the short-run macroeconomic stabilisation policies slow growth, indicating a transitional cost, although the negative effect disappears over the long run. Lensink and Morrissey (1999) argue that to the extent that it is linked with volatility and unpredictability of aid flows, conditionality is itself a major source of macroeconomic instability in poor countries dependent on aid to finance current expenditures. The stop-go financing associated with loan conditionality leads to greater uncertainty, thus reducing the effectiveness of both aid and changes in policies.

Easterly (2003) revisits the Burnside and Dollar study using alternative specifications by taking averages of the dependent growth variable over longer periods than in the original study, on the grounds that aid could affect growth more over long periods of good policy than over short ones (Burnside and Dollar use average per capita growth figures over four-year periods; Easterly used periods of 8, 12 and 24 years). Easterly concludes that the result that aid boosts growth in good policy environments depends on defining growth, aid and policy over a sufficiently short period. Alternative period lengths from one to 12 years and for the whole 24 years, using a dataset extended from that employed by Burnside and Dollar, all yielded insignificant results on the interactive term between aid and policy.

Joyce (2006) draws attention to some undesirable characteristics of good compliers with conditionality. She studies the determinants of the degree of IMF programme implementation and finds that countries less open to trade, with governments longer in power and with less democratic political regimes, tend to have better rates of implementation. Dreher (2006) finds that economic growth tends to be lower in countries with IMF loans and programmes in place. Moreover, he uses three different measures of compliance, each of which has a negative coefficient when included individually. In his review paper, Dreher (2008, p. 30) concludes that there is little evidence that IMF conditionality helps governments to commit to their own preferred policies. Conditions do provide a valuable signal and reduce moral hazard, but there is no evidence that they help the IMF to safeguard its resources.

ISBN: 978-92-64-07551-1 © OECD 2009

Mosley *et al.* (2004) study the criteria for aid disbursement. They find that donors assign aid according to the perceived quality of a recipient's macroeconomic policy (measured as performance on inflation and the budget deficit), suggesting some sensitivity to the adoption of good policies. Nevertheless, the macro-policy variable has a very small coefficient (0.096), suggesting only a marginal role in the allocation of aid. Easterly (2007) also looks at this issue and finds, in line with the basic precepts of the *New Aid Agenda* and the Paris Declaration, some weak evidence that aid agencies are increasingly sensitive to recipient-country needs (in terms of per capita income, poverty alleviation, etc.).

Notes

1. The MONA database itself is not free of problems. Only programmes which have been reviewed by the Executive Board are included in the database – programmes that are interrupted or permanently cancelled are not covered, something which might overstate compliance in any econometric analysis based on this dataset. In addition, coverage does not go back far enough to allow for longer-term empirical analysis (Dreher, 2008, p. 23).

2. The finding of the World Bank's independent commission into the quality of its research (the Deaton Commission) is especially revealing on some of the weaknesses of the Burnside and Dollar study, and is worth quoting at length. There the authors note that: "In spite of having been published in the *American Economic Review*, the Burnside and Dollar paper is unconvincing. The analysis uses an index of policy that combines the government surplus, the inflation rate, and an openness measure, at least two of which are measures of outcomes, not of policies (as is indeed recognised in later work by Collier and Dollar). It is also clear from the way in which this index is constructed that the results are not robust; attempts to work with all three measures fail, as does a principal components index, and the final index is constructed using a regression of growth on policy that is at best arbitrary, and at worst appears to be inconsistent with the main equation of interest. But this issue is dwarfed by the spectre that haunts all of this literature, that external aid is not only a determinant of economic performance, but is determined by it. ... Again, we are not arguing that the Burnside and Dollar paper is weaker than most of the literature on aid effectiveness, but we are arguing that its results provide only the weakest of evidence for their central contention, that aid is effective when policies are sound." (Deaton *et al.*, 2006, p. 53-54).

ISBN: 978-92-64-07551-1 © OECD 2009

Chapter 5

The Intrinsic Difficulty of Distinguishing Between Good and Bad Policies

A surprising consensus now exists among economists that there is "no one way to do things." As far back as 1979, the IMF's Guidelines on Conditionality stressed the need to avoid blueprint approaches, pay due regard to individual political and economic circumstances of particular countries, and keep the number of conditions attached to loans to a minimum. The World Bank (2005, p. 22) recognised in its 2005 *Conditionality Review* that "the lessons of the 1990s show that generalised policy prescriptions often fail, and that there is no single model of development." Such declarations cut across ideological divides. Stiglitz (2005, p. 1) observes "if there is a consensus today about what strategies are likely to help the development of the poorest countries it is this: there is no consensus." Feldstein (1998, p. 5) makes a similar point:

"Imposing detailed economic prescriptions on legitimate governments would remain questionable even if economists were unanimous about the best way to reform the countries' economic policies. In practice, however, there are substantial disagreements about what should be done."

Notwithstanding declarations like these, which have now become commonplace, the economics profession arguably still tends towards excessively reductionist and prescriptive approaches to economic problems. Underlying this is the basic methodological approach to which most economists ascribe: it is difficult to reconcile the search for universal rules which govern economic phenomena with the idea that a broad palette of effective development strategies exists. And the issue is important because professional economists often heavily influence the formulation of policy towards developing countries.

One could take these arguments further and argue that the ideals of good governance and good policies are flawed by their essentially ephemeral character. In economic policy making "good" and "bad" are words that express current value judgements of individuals, interest groups and entire polities. Thus, no immutable set of policies deemed "good" can exist; any consensus changes over time. The Washington Consensus, thought definitive when first elaborated in 1989, offers a good illustration: it has subsequently seen substantial modification, and some people now speak, tongue in cheek, of a post-post Washington Consensus (Table 5.1)[1].

Table 5.1. **The Washington Consensus and the Augmented Washington Consensus**

Original Washington Consensus	"Augmented" Washington Consensus: the previous ten items, plus:
1. Fiscal discipline	11. Corporate governance
2. Reorientation of public expenditures	12. Anti-corruption
3. Tax reform	13. Flexible labour markets
4. Financial liberalisation	14. WTO agreements
5. Unified and competitive exchange rates	15. Financial codes and standards
6. Trade liberalisation	16. "Prudent" capital-account opening
7. Openness to FDI	17. Non-intermediate exchange rate regimes
8. Privatisation	18. Independent central banks/inflation targeting
9. Deregulation	19. Social safety nets
10.Secure Property Rights	20. Targeted poverty reduction

Source: Rodrik (2006).

Given its import for debates on conditionality and the delineation of the "right set of policies", this point is worth dwelling on. Even when there has been near unanimity about appropriate economic policies, the consensus has changed radically (Feldstein, 1998, p. 5). The IMF, for instance, was created to defend and manage a fixed exchange-rate system now regarded as economically inappropriate and practically unworkable, yet it still plays a key role in a transformed international monetary system. Similarly, for a long time, advice to developing countries from the World Bank, the Economic Commission for Latin America and the Caribbean (ECLAC) and leading academic specialists emphasised national plans for government-managed industrial development. Now the consensus urges opposite policies: flexible exchange rates, market-determined economic development and free trade. As we shall see in Chapter 8, the current financial crisis has made these inconsistencies even more self-evident.

ISBN: 978-92-64-07551-1 © OECD 2009

All this puts professional economists in a difficult position with regard to issuing policy advice. Tarp (2001, p. 342), for instance, concedes that he has "always been worried about being caught up in the latest World Bank fads. The boundary between policy advocacy and policy research is not always clearly delineated and over the years we have seen many shifts of direction and emphasis in the policy advice and lending emanating from the World Bank". One notorious example of how the donor community has done a u-turn on policy was the pressure placed on many low-income countries in the 1980s and 1990s to introduce user fees in health and education services, a policy now widely recognised as extremely counterproductive. Donors on the one hand acknowledged the importance of expanding social expenditures and on the other obliged countries to undertake "fiscal tightening" – a difficult task to reconcile in any case. But then, through the introduction of fees, they pursued policies which ultimately restricted the access of the poor to those very same services. By 1995, 28 of 37 countries in Africa had introduced fees for basic healthcare. As late as 1998 some 75 per cent of World Bank loans to Africa still included the establishment or expansion of user fees. In Zimbabwe, the use of health facilities fell by 25 per cent in three years following the introduction of user fees, while child mortality rose by 13 per cent. The effect was similar in Ghana, the Democratic Republic of Congo, Swaziland and Lesotho (Glennie, 2008, p. 43). Acknowledgement of error and a subsequent change of policy is of course a positive thing, especially when adapting to new circumstances. Indeed, few policy frameworks shift more frequently than aid policies. But the fact that this received wisdom changes so often should at the very least provide the motivation for a serious reassessment of policy conditionality.

Giving more policy space to the developing countries themselves would surely be a better approach. As the communiqué made at the G8 summit at Gleaneagles in 2005 suggested, "it is up to developing countries themselves and their governments to take the lead on development. They need to decide, plan and sequence their economic policies to fit their own development strategies, for which they should be accountable to all their people" (cited by UNCTAD, 2008, p. 93). Yet according to the World Bank (2007), no least developed country (LDC) yet has a "sustainable" operational development strategy and only six of the 37 LDCs have "largely developed" ones[2]. And although PRSPs fall far short of comprehensive development plans, it is in any case somewhat ironic that donors and the IFIs now promote "development strategies" when much of their effort in the 1980s and 1990s worked against the idea of any kind of planning, and that to most mainstream economists planning has become an anathema.

ISBN: 978-92-64-07551-1 © OECD 2009

The difficulties surrounding indexes like the World Bank's Country Policy and Institutional Assessments (CPIAs) illustrate the intrinsic problems of determining when policy is "good" or not. The CPIAs are used as guides for concessional lending policies (most notably by the International Development Association [IDA]) and many analysts consider them among the most carefully constructed sets of governance indicators. Bank staff follow specific guidelines to rate and benchmark countries in each region. They currently assess and rate 16 policy and institutional performance areas every year, grouped and averaged into four clusters: *i)* economic management; *ii)* social inclusion and equity; *iii)* public sector management and institutions; and *iv)* structural reform policies.

As a key tool in the application of conditionality, it would be foolish to underestimate the importance of the CPIA. The World Bank's CPIA has also been used as a model for other development banks, such as the African Development Bank which now produces its own CPIA, and many other donors use the World Bank's analysis to make their own decisions about where to target aid. As a consequence, if a country scores well on the CPIA criteria it is likely to see aid increase – if it scores badly, it will find it harder to access funds. In this way, the CPIA inadvertently contributes to creating the cleavage between "aid darlings" and "aid orphans". According to the World Bank's own data (IDA, 2003, p. 8) the countries in the top performance quintile ("strong performers") received on average four to five times more IDA aid per capita than the countries classified in the bottom quintile ("poor performers"). Another major shortcoming for aid recipients has resided in the CPIAs' lack of transparency. Until 2006, the scores given to particular countries remained secret and confidential to the World Bank (Arndt and Oman, 2006, p. 40; Riddell, 2007, p. 234). More pointedly, perhaps, only fairly ambiguous correlations appear between economic growth and the various components of the CPIA, particularly public-sector management and institutions (Figure 5.1), suggesting some serious limitations in the CPIAs as tools for measuring policy effectiveness, even on traditional grounds of generating economic growth, let alone for achieving poverty reduction or human development.

ISBN: 978-92-64-07551-1 © OECD 2009

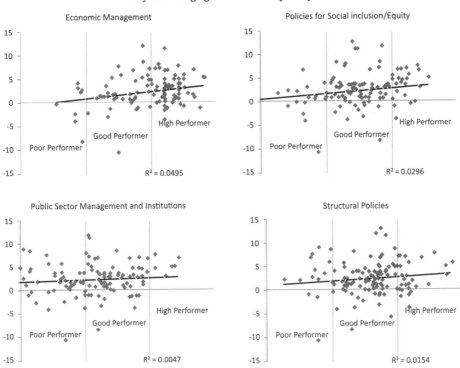

Figure 5.1 **GDP per Capita Growth and Country Performance (CPIA)**
by Policy Area, FY1996-2001
3 year average growth in GDP per capita

Source: World Bank (2007, p. 189).

One fundamental issue not addressed in the elaboration of policy performance indexes like the CPIA is the correct sequencing of policy implementation. Poor economies suffer from a variety of afflictions related to poor human capital endowments, the ineffective use of capital and other resources, poor institutions, unstable fiscal and monetary policies, inadequate private incentives for investment and technology adoption, poor access to credit, poor integration with world markets and so on. Rodrik (2007, p. 89) emphasises, "To say that one has to overcome all these disadvantages in order to develop is at once a tautology and quite unhelpful…the trick is to find those areas where reform will yield the greatest return, or where we can get the biggest bang for the reform buck. What we need to know, in other words, is where the most binding constraint to growth lies." In the tradition of the second-best theorem, the theoretically best solution to a given economic problem may not always provide the biggest welfare payoff[3]. It is thus important to analyse the possible trade-offs between different policy options. Yet donors often refrain from doing so, preferring simply to identify long lists of policy requirements (what is sometimes referred to as "the laundry-list approach" to policy making). For example, in the late 1990s, the World Bank, an organisation with "plenty of ideas but no priorities", set 111 conditions in its policy framework paper for Kenya alone, a trend which Edwards (1999, p. 118) describes as "conditionality gone mad". World Bank economists Pritchett and Woolcock (2004, p. 192) make some particularly adroit observations on this issue:

> "Most agree the debate about the Washington consensus is blown far out of proportion. At times 90 per cent of the ink spilled addresses 10 per cent of the development battle; in the end, no matter who is right about trade policy, fiscal deficits and the like, these policies do not add up to anything like a complete development agenda .... Policies such as trade openness, fiscal probity, etc. need to be seen as part of, not a substitute for, a coherent development strategy. Even the 'augmented Washington consensus' that adds the provision of some key services (such as education) to the standard policy agenda leaves wide open the standard policy question of how things will actually be accomplished. In general economists have focused their tools on the question of what governments should do, with relatively less attention given to the economics and politics of how to accomplish the 'what'."

In a generally overlooked, but deeply insightful book, Atul Kohli (2004, p. 12) notes that:

> "The nearly exclusive focus in the literature on appropriate policy choices is incomplete, even misleading. Policy choices matter, of course, but these choices must be explained. More important, the impact of the same policy applied in two different settings may vary because of the contextual differences, some of the more obvious being varying global conditions and different initial conditions of an economy."

From this point of view, there is no one correct or incorrect policy. As the *New Aid Agenda* fortunately recognises increasingly, implementation is key. If this diagnosis is right, development policy must engage in realistic evaluations of policy options – in other words, a return to political economy. Peter Nolan (2004, p. 97) argues quite rightly that, "Far too often, economic advice has been little more than slogans. Too rarely has it consisted of careful, pragmatic political economy". This implies that policy conditionality has become largely obsolete and that donors need to explore other ways to maximise the efficiency of their aid money.

ISBN: 978-92-64-07551-1 © OECD 2009

Notes

1. The intellectual confusion around the relationship between policy and development is revealed by the contradictions evident in the overview to a major World Bank study (Devarajan *et al.*, 2001). On page 2 the authors claim that "we know enough about development policies to make a fair assessment of the quality of policies across countries and over time", but this affirmation squares particularly badly with the admission on page 33 that "we simply do not know what is good policy, and the issue for donors is to support genuine policy learning rather than to impose models through conditionality".

2. These countries are Burkina Faso, Ethiopia, Rwanda, Tanzania, Uganda and Zambia.

3. As Toye (1993, p. 96) explains, intuitively one can see that unless an economy suffers from only one distortion, or departure from the requirements for perfectly competitive behaviour, there is no guarantee that removing the distortion would produce an increase in welfare. Two or more distortions might partially or wholly cancel each other out, and thus their removal might make the economy more inefficient than it was before. As Toye notes, "given that, in the real world, economies rarely suffer from just a single distortion, the theorem seems to mean that there is no way of knowing whether piecemeal attempts to introduce perfectly competitive markets will raise or lower welfare. The second-best theorem seems to lead to policy agnosticism".

Chapter 6

The Slippery Slope of Political Conditionality

The effectiveness of conditionality hinges in large measure on the willingness of donors to suspend aid in the case of non-compliance. Yet, for a multitude of reasons, donors often hesitate (Killick, 1998; Kanbur, 2000; Woods, 2007; Dreher, 2008). Donor governments have historical, foreign policy, security, investment and trading reasons to support particular recipient governments and to use their aid and their influence within the IFIs to secure lenient treatment for favoured clients. Economic and geopolitical considerations still go a long way in explaining the geographic allocation of aid flows. Indeed, the diplomatic use of aid undoubtedly received a boost from the terrorist attack of 9/11, with aid flows to the Middle East increasing four-fold between 2001 and 2004 (Lancaster, 2007, p. 7). Against this backdrop, donors are often reluctant to cut aid, regardless of how recipients have scored in achieving targets and objectives. As Kanbur puts it (2000, pp. 5-6), "When push comes to shove, all of the pressures, mostly from the donor side, are to look the other way when conditionality is violated." Moreover, the instruments of donor co-ordination are only on rare occasions strong enough to maintain solidarity in the face of conflicting donor interests (Killick, 1998, p. 174). And clever recipient governments often adopt effective divide-and-rule strategies towards donors.

Donor agencies' self interest also often argues against imposing the sanction of aid withdrawal because of the imperative to keep relations with recipients on an even footing. Implementing sanctions implies putting future aid projects and programmes in jeopardy, on which depend the livelihoods and careers of agency staff as well as the image of an agency in the eyes of its political masters. This creates implicit pressure to keep the aid flowing (Kanbur, 2000, p. 6). In a final paradox, pressures to continue aid flows in spite of non-compliance derive partly from the very power that donors hold over budgets of many developing country governments. The poorest members of society may suffer directly from the cutback in aid, leaving the ruling elite relatively untouched. Under such circumstances, the consequences of cutting funds can make bad situations worse and could easily turn them into public relations liabilities for the donors. Thus aid engenders a kind of moral hazard (some call it a *Samaritan's Dilemma*) where donor support becomes too crucial to let the country fail.

Together, these points imply a very serious difficulty in actually applying conditionality, undermining its whole rationale. Some realistic hypothetical examples can drive this point home:

1) In country A, the government shows good signs of being on track towards the MDGs and has made a lot of progress in areas such as primary education and health. Nevertheless, there are increasing signs of authoritarian behaviour on the part of the president, with the government locking up many opposition members. Widespread demonstrations and strikes have occurred in response, with protesters killed in the subsequent repression. Opposition members in exile urge the withdrawal of aid to the government. How should the donor community respond?

2) In country B, the government presides over a fragile but functioning democracy. The MDGs are not being attained, however, in part because of resource pilfering and extreme corruption. The country is a key western ally in its region, and international security issues are at stake. Should the donor community curtail aid?

3) In country C, after rising dissatisfaction with reforms, a new populist government comes to power promising to renege on international debt commitments and to reverse the reforms. Tensions with major western powers rise, and ambassadors are expelled. Several major private-sector projects are cancelled. The donor community currently funds many worthwhile projects tackling poverty, and some NGOs endorse the new government's stance. Should donors cut aid?

4) Country D has a deplorable record on human rights. Illiteracy and child mortality rates are among the highest in the world. The current president has been in power for over 30 years, since he took power in a *coup d'état*. Ten years ago, significant oil deposits were found. A number of industrial countries re-evaluated the situation, strengthened their diplomatic ties and initiated aid programmes. Should industrial-country donors follow the herd?

ISBN: 978-92-64-07551-1 © OECD 2009

These hypothetical examples demonstrate how conditionality is contingent on political realities. Development professionals and government officials may define conditionality technically and as objectively as they can, but political realities often override their appraisals. Aid programmes rarely have management freedom independent of broader political realities. Governments have sets of interests in their foreign relations – political, military and economic – and development aid remains subordinate to those interests if conflicts of interest arise, as we shall see in the following section.

Yet most donors are still reluctant to accept the idea that they impose "political conditionality" (Baylies, 1995), preferring the more acceptable terms of "democracy promotion" or "governance" conditionalities. Democracy promotion was largely unheard of during the Cold War. It was only with the collapse of the Soviet Union that western countries felt confident enough to pursue not only economic but also democratisation goals through their aid programmes. Buiter (2004) points out that all process conditionality (where donors try to impose certain ways of carrying out policies or decision taking) is in fact political or governance conditionality, with sometimes only a fine line between the two. For instance, of 20 criteria applied by the World Bank and the African Development Bank in annual CPIA to determine eligibility for aid, six criteria concern governance. These cover matters such as anti-corruption, property rights, tax collection and public consent for policies (Sogge, 2002, p. 132).

Donors have different constraints and embrace different policies on these issues. For example, the European Union sets its development co-operation explicitly within the framework of its overall political relationships (DFID, 2005, p. 14). The IMF and World Bank Articles of Agreement require them to link lending conditions to their eventual economic impact and in theory prevent them from using political conditionality. As noted in Chapter 2, however, political conditionality in some shape or form has often seeped into IFI lending, starting right back with the World Bank's first loan in 1947 to France. The European Bank of Reconstruction and Development (EBRD), in contrast, has long practised process conditionality because of the expressly political nature of its mandate, which in that regard is unlike that of the other IFIs.

Conditionality has sometimes gone far beyond the endorsement of specific policies or processes; donors on occasions have tried to influence institutions and personnel as well (Krasner, 1999, p. 147). The World Bank began as early as the 1950s to encourage the creation of agencies within national governments that would be insulated from domestic political pressures and be more responsive to their own policy preferences. In the past, the World Bank has also pushed for the creation of planning agencies and a corps of technocrats. It has paid for foreign consultants in ministries and government agencies and has had veto power over the choices of consultants. The IMF has often had representatives in the central banks of client states, with access to government records and files. Some of these measures became increasingly personal. For example, in the run-up to the Enhanced Structural Adjustment Policy (ESAF) in Madagascar in 1995, the main conditionality imposed was the sacking of the central bank governor, Raoul Ravelomana (Mosley and Eeckhout, 2000, p. 142).

Ironically enough, political or governance conditionality shifts attention toward coherence of donor rather than recipient policy. Do donors disburse aid in line with the high-minded principles they espouse? Broadly speaking, the answer is "No". Econometric studies show quite clearly that despite the boldness of donor proclamations on political conditionality, aid has remained quite unresponsive to good governance. Svensson (2000) finds no evidence that donors systematically allocate aid to countries with less corruption. Alesina and Weder (2002) find no significant correlation between levels of corruption and the allocation of foreign aid, regardless of the period under consideration. They note no apparent change in donor behaviour since the 1990s, although they present some evidence that political interests might have played a smaller role in the 1990s than previously (the variables "years as a colony" and "Israel" are no longer significant) (Table 6.1). Similarly, the authors study the factors which impinge on debt relief (a major component of overall aid flows) and find no evidence that debt relief programmes have been targeted to less corrupt countries. At the same time, the indicator of openness (a proxy for desirable economic policies) loses its previous significance in the 1990s. Easterly (2007) runs similar regressions on data from 1980 to 2003 and does find a slightly significant increase of democracy as a determinant of aid flows after 1990 as well as more significant coefficients on corruption after 1995, but notes that the significance mostly disappears in 2000-03.

ISBN: 978-92-64-07551-1 © OECD 2009

Table 6.1. **Official Foreign Aid, Political Rights Corruption: OLS Panel Regressions of Five-Year Averages (dependent variable: log of aid per capita)**

Independent Variable	Period		
	1975-95	1980-90	1990-95
Constant	14.58	15.93	14.59
	(5.73)	(7.77)	(2.70)
Log Initial Income Per Capita	-0.56	-0.67	-0.67
	(-4.99)	(-4.31)	(-3.55)
Log Population	-0.62	-0.63	-0.53
	(-13.44)	(-12.48)	(-7.37)
Openness	0.53	0.67	0.31
	(3.24)	(2.66)	(1.29)
Political Rights	-0.03	-0.06	0.05
	(-0.85)	(-1.02)	(0.67)
Years as Colony	0.01	0.00	0.00
	(2.85)	(1.72)	(0.77)
Friend of United States	0.01	0.001	0.001
	(0.70)	(0.07)	(0.04)
Egypt	2.18	1.83	1.97
	(9.77)	(15.67)	(7.62)
Israel	2.69	3.08	3.40
	(2.18)	(3.27)	(1.01)
Corruption	-0.02	0.05	-0.05
	(-0.39)	(0.67)	(-0.44)
Time Dummies	yes	no	no
Adjusted R^2	0.65	0.65	0.69
Observations	269	137	64

Notes: Values in parenthesis are t statistics. Standard errors are calculated using White correction

Source: Alesina and Weder (2002, p. 1132)

StatLink ▓▒░ http://dx.doi.org/10.1787/704138803015

Donors have not even always strictly practised fiduciary conditionality – the most basic requirement for effective aid delivery. At the World Bank, for instance, one estimate (Winters, 2002, p. 101) says that roughly USD 100 billion of its loan funds intended for development went missing in its first 50 years of operations through loans to corrupt governments (Zaire under Mobutu [now the Democratic Republic of Congo] and Indonesia in Suharto's time provide the best-known examples). There is evidence too about the way in which IMF finance has been pilfered in the past. In the case of Zaire, despite Mobutu's miserable record, between 1976 and 1989 major creditor countries rescheduled its debt no fewer than nine times. In 1987 a senior IMF official resigned over the extension of a new loan, claiming that there had been too much political meddling in favour of Zaire's government (Wrong, 2002).

When econometric analyses distinguish between donors, Easterly (2007, p. 658) finds that the World Bank shows no sign of increased sensitivity towards policies or corruption despite the policy revolution it led after 1980. According to Alesina and Weder (2002), whereas the Scandinavian countries and Australia give more to less corrupt governments, corruption correlates positively with aid received from the United States. Berthélemy (2006) provides a similar breakdown of donor motivations, distinguishing between "altruistic" and "egotistical" countries in terms of both the extent to which trade and aid are interrelated and the degree to which a donor's priorities differ from those of an "average" donor. Altruistic behaviour implies aid decisions made independently of the specific relations that exist between donors and recipients. The most altruistic donors are Austria, Ireland, the Netherlands, New Zealand, Norway and Switzerland. The egotistical cluster includes Australia, France, Italy, the United States and Japan. Other evidence (e.g. Andersen *et al.*, 2006) shows that even the IFIs, which pride themselves on their supposedly apolitical and technocratic approach to aid, often align closely with the foreign policy objectives of their major benefactors. One sees little sign, then, of a shift towards more ethical or discriminating aid policies. In other words, conditionality has had little or no impact on actual outcomes, despite what the contemporary rhetoric suggests as desirable *a priori*.

Qualitative studies bolster this conclusion. In his study of IMF policy, Killick (1985, p. 189-90) noted a surprising degree of arbitrary fixing of IMF conditions. The IMF has always said officially that a government must design a detailed programme to strengthen the balance of payments and that the Fund did not seek to become involved in the details of proposals concerning taxation, government expenditure and the like. The reality proved more complex, however, with much depending on the key personalities on both sides of the table, on past relations with the IMF and on the gravity of the economic situation: "Politicking by executive directors and others is a chief reason for the Fund's inability to achieve uniformity of treatment across countries….Countries lacking in geo-political importance are the chief sufferers, whatever the hue of their governments." (Killick, 1985, p. 221). In the mid-1990s, the IMF abandoned lending limits related to quota size, allowing for larger support packages "in exceptional circumstances". Buira (2003, p. 75) notes how in practice, such exceptions have been made for significant emerging-market economies in which

ISBN: 978-92-64-07551-1 © OECD 2009

foreign portfolio investors have a large stake – for example, Turkey's maximum access in excess of 1 700 per cent of quota in 2003. The 1997 stand-by agreement with South Korea received wide criticism for including bilateral trade conditions tailored to benefit American and Japanese companies. Discretion also facilitates the promotion of geopolitical interests. According to Buira, Executive Directors and borrowing governments widely understand that strategically placed nations such as Turkey and Afghanistan will much more likely receive sympathetic consideration than geopolitically less important nations.

More crucially, for large countries with relatively minor dependence on aid flows (e.g. China or Indonesia) conditionality has always been a fairly futile exercise. Conditionality will not work under any circumstances when the implications of abandoning a country to its fate are simply too onerous for the international community to assume (Mold, 2007). This was the case with Mexico's IMF bailout after the financial collapse of 1994 and is perhaps true now for Ethiopia, considered as a bulwark of relative stability in an otherwise conflict-ridden, terrorist-infiltrated region. Effectively, conditionality often applies only to countries either too weak to resist or bereft of geostrategic importance – hardly a fair application of development principles.

Chapter 7

Conditionality and the Shift to New Aid Modalities: How Far Does Budget Support Resolve the Dilemma?

Having established the practical difficulties of allocating aid according to performance, in this Chapter we ask the question about how donors can limit the difficulties associated with conditionality. Arguably, part of the solution entails re-examining the arguments in favour of different aid modalities. OECD (2008*b*, p. 15) points out that most donors mix aid modalities depending on local contexts, with no one preferred way of delivering aid. Many donors still rely on project aid, whether or not as part of sector or programme approaches, to maintain contact with field realities, to work with non-traditional actors such as the private sector and civil society, to develop innovative approaches and to compensate for weak national capacity. The proliferation of decentralised co-operation, especially in donor countries such as Spain which have expanded their co-operation significantly in recent years, has increased the visibility of project aid.

As noted in Chapter 2, the 1960s and 1970s were the golden age of project aid – aid that was generally disbursed with a low degree of conditionality. It involved conditionality limited to the specific project rather than the general policies of the recipient country. Typical conditions embodied in project agreements included commitments by recipient governments to provide local finance or otherwise cofinance projects, to make complementary investments (e.g. roads to enable agricultural output from irrigation projects to be marketed) and to provide budgetary resources for project operation and maintenance after completion. "Such project conditionality – which also applies to bilateral project aid – was taken for granted and not questioned" (Singer and Raffer, 1996, p. 153).

The period of project-led aid led to mixed results. Many developing countries clearly failed to make the social and economic transformations that they hoped for, despite large injections of foreign aid. Nevertheless, the developing world's growth record during this period was unprecedented, and development finance notched up some important successes over the period, such as the remarkable turnaround in agricultural production during the Green Revolution in India between 1967, when it was the world's second largest cereal importer, and 1979, when it produced enough food to feed its population (Caulfield, 1996, p. 111).

Moreover, some authors (e.g. Rich, 2002; Singer and Raffer, 1996) suggest that the subsequent shift to policy-conditional programme lending itself reduced the quality of project lending. The *Wapenhams Report* (World Bank, 1992), an authoritative document written from inside the World Bank and published in 1992, provided evidence that the number and proportion of faulty World Bank project loans sharply increased after policy-conditional programme lending was introduced. The report found that over one-third of completed projects became failures by the Bank's own criteria and well over half of ongoing operations (over three-quarters in sub-Saharan Africa) did not have "likely sustainability". Singer and Raffer (*op. cit.*) argue that the shift of expertise needed within the World Bank was largely responsible for these failures: efficient technicians are required for project work – irrigation engineers, sanitation experts and so on, whereas for programme lending and the associated policy conditionality macroeconomists are more in demand. But the two types of approach and work are not easily combined in the same institution, and macroeconomists clearly saw their position strengthened with the rise of conditionality, to the neglect of the more operational day-to-day work of more technical careers.

According to Mosley and Eeckhout (2000), problems with project aid became increasingly evident even prior to the debt crisis of the 1980s in the so-called *micro-macro paradox*, where quite respectable rates of return on individual projects were accompanied with disappointing macroeconomic results. Nevertheless, the switch away from project to programme aid had little to do with these problems, but was rather an expedient reaction by donors to the challenges created by the debt crisis: donors needed a quick-disbursing aid instrument that could bring about policy change and would build government capacity depleted by the stabilisation measures of the 1980s. Project aid, it was decided, could do none of these things (Mosley and Eeckhout, 2000, p. 136). Another motive driving the move away from project aid was the objective of reducing the transaction costs of providing aid, which had been rising sharply (Riddell, 2007, p. 201). The traditional critique of project aid is well summarised

ISBN: 978-92-64-07551-1 © OECD 2009

by Killick (2008, p. 4): "Traditional assistance can lead to a proliferation of projects which is incoherent, non-transparent and inconsistent with the national government's priorities. Project aid also spawns large numbers of Project Implementation Units (PIUs), often outside the government's structures, tending to weaken efforts to build capacities within the public service. More generally, assistance programmes are often not well aligned with national development strategies, institutions and procedures."

As a consequence in the last two decades we have witnessed a marked shift towards ambitious and innovative forms of programme aid – that is, any form of contributions made available to a recipient's country for general development purposes and which is not tied to specific projects, such as balance-of-payments support, general budget support, commodity assistance or debt relief. In the last decade, in particular, many hopes in particular have been pinned on budget support. As one study explains:

"There is a wide range of expectations from general budget support. These include: improved co-ordination and harmonisation among donors; alignment with partner country systems and policies; lower transaction costs; higher allocative efficiency of public expenditure; greater predictability of funding; increased effectiveness of the state and public administration as general budget support is aligned with and uses government allocation and financial management systems; and improved domestic accountability through increased focus on the government's own accountability channels" (IDD and Associates, 2006, p. 1).

Yet despite a strong *a priori* rationale, the empirical evidence for the superiority of some of the new aid modalities over old-fashioned project aid remains quite weak. On budget support, the few impact studies undertaken so far all have conceptual and methodological problems stemming chiefly from the difficulty of tracing the effects on poverty and income levels of adding aid to overall budgetary resources (Riddell, 2007, p. 201). Further complications arise because budget support may constitute only a relatively small proportion of total aid resources; its impact is difficult to disentangle from that delivered through other aid modalities.

Some important lessons can be gleaned from past experiences. In spite of the impression often given of budget support as an innovatory modality of aid delivery, it is not by any stretch of the imagination new. The Marshall Plan was essentially an ambitious (and by almost all accounts successful) experiment in budget support, though arguably under very special conditions – the reconstruction of countries which had already attained relatively high levels of institutional and human development. Subsequent experiences have been far more mixed. The United Kingdom provided budget support to a number of former African economies in the wake of independence during the 1960s, but gradually phased this out in favour of projects. In the 1990s, there were a number of experiments in budget support in Bangladesh, Cape Verde, Nicaragua and Tanzania. Again the experiences were mainly mixed and conditionality quite pervasive in the implemented programmes (White and Dijkstra, 2003). Most Australian aid to Papua New Guinea from its independence in 1975 until the mid-1990s also took the form of budget support. The Australian government estimated the total disbursements up to the early 2000s at USD 14 billion, so the sums were enormous. Yet an extensive official Australian evaluation carried out in 2003 heavily criticised the results, especially in terms of the accepted primary objective of budget support – increasing the autonomy and capacity of national institutions (AusAid, 2003). The report concluded (p. xi) "In considering the impact of aid since independence, it is relevant to recognise that there was a clear rationale for budget support in the immediate post-independence period but, in time, it was recognised that budget support had an adverse impact on incentives to develop and implement effective economic development policies."

One of the most extensive recent evaluations of budget support has been a three-year study commissioned by a consortium of donors in 2003, at the request of the OECD. It involved development of a methodology to evaluate budget support and case studies in seven countries: Burkina Faso, Malawi, Mozambique, Nicaragua, Rwanda, Uganda and Viet Nam. The published report (IDD and Associates, 2006) endorsed budget support but had mixed conclusions on its effectiveness. On the positive side, it found that funding of basic public services in health and education increased during the provision of budget support and found some evidence of reduced transaction costs of multiple meetings, donor visits and reporting requirements. But it also found under-estimation of the political risks in several countries, with over-optimistic assumptions about the ability of international partners to influence matters deeply rooted in partner countries' political systems. It also drew attention to some fundamental tensions regarding the desire of donors to establish benchmarks and controls, their temptation to indulge in micromanagement and recipient countries' wish to enjoy maximum liberty to determine expenditures according to their own priorities. The risk that budget support could paradoxically actually end up strengthening donor interference and control over recipient governments was spelled out very clearly by White and Dijkstra (2003, p. 550):

ISBN: 978-92-64-07551-1 © OECD 2009

"In most countries there is an enormous scope for improvement in public financial management, in budget reporting procedures and in accountability of budget performance to parliament and to the public at large. If donors succeed in focusing on these issues...and if they succeed in harmonising and simplifying their procedures with regard to budget support, these positive systemic effects become a reality. *However, if they attempt to micro-manage the use of the funds and if each donor continues to set is specific requirements for that use or for reporting, budget support will become a drag on development.*"

It is not clear yet whether donors have managed to avoid these problems. In their study of the Multi-Donor Budget Support for Ghana, Killick and Lawson (2007, p. 4) note that "it has not achieved a sufficient critical mass and it has strayed too far from its initial objective of reducing transactions costs. These flaws have prevented it from minimising the risks of injecting budget support into a still weak fiscal system. While it is seen as having kept reform on the agenda and as having a generally pro-poor influence, it has neither been able to minimise the risks by galvanising more effective *Performance Finance Management* (PFM) systems nor to maximise the payoff in terms of poverty-reduction." A UK Parliamentary Committee (Committee of Public Accounts, 2008, pp. 5-7) into the use of budgetary support by DFID arrived at the conclusion that the decision process governing which countries receive budget support is still opaque: "DFID have stated principles which must be met before working with government partners, and have developed useful tools to help appraise prospects for budget support and assess risks. Most budget support proposals, however, do not clearly weigh up the risks and benefits. In addition, the pattern of budget support that has arisen appears arbitrary."

Knoll (2008, p. 12) notes that the donor community, which includes bilateral development agencies, the European Commission (EC) and regional development banks, still views recipient compliance with the terms of the IDA's *Poverty Reduction Support Credit* (PRSC) and the IMF's *Poverty Reduction and Growth Facility* as a precondition for general budget support disbursal. Among the bilateral agencies, for instance, SIDA (Sweden) directly or indirectly (via the EC) attaches its release decision to recipient compliance with PRGF conditionality, and makes decisions on a case-by-case basis. The Belgian budget-support scheme for Burkina Faso is attached to *Poverty Reduction Support Credit* conditionality, while DFID (United Kingdom) draws its disbursal conditions from the PRSP (or from the terms of the PRGF, if those are considered consistent with the British approach). In the United Republic of Tanzania, DANIDA (Denmark) partly referred to PRSC prior actions but also took into consideration conditions directly from the PRSP. Linking up budget support to IFI programmes means that, despite the intentions of budget support, conditionality is still pervasive.

As a consequence of all this, the strengthening of domestic accountability remains an elusive objective (de Renzio, 2006). It would seem reasonable to conclude that budget support is still far from delivering in terms of its promise to reduce conditionality and enhance recipient country ownership. Moreover, it appears to be particularly unsuited to fragile states with weak institutional structures. If that is the case, then there is a danger that it ends up legitimising a new kind of *ex ante* conditionality, whereby budget support is considered appropriate for some countries, but not for others. In a sense, then, it is open to the same criticisms described in Box 1.2 regarding the Millennium Challenge Account. In addition, because of its all-encompassing nature, budget support, however well designed, almost inevitably leaves an enormous amount of discretion to donors in terms of deciding whether a country is progressing well or not, and thus is worthy of continued support. This puts recipient governments constantly on the defensive, in terms of justifying their performance, and raises the risk, paradoxically, of greater conditionality, not less. It has led to a situation whereby donors demand greater participation in policy discussions and planning in a number of countries, and become deeply involved in core policy processes. Donors have also lacked important political economy insights as to the nature of domestic power struggles. Precisely for these reasons, there has been a growing number of voices questioning the wisdom of a greater emphasis on budget support (de Renzio, 2006; Deaton *et al.*, 2006; Whitfield and Maipose, 2008; de Renzio and Hanlon, 2009)[1]. Disappointing or politically complicated experiences of budget support in recent years with previously designated aid "darlings" (countries such as Ethiopia, Rwanda and Uganda) have also convinced some members of the donor community to stay on the sidelines for the time being: they have either set a ceiling to this aid modality (25 per cent in the case of Denmark) or still make little use (Canada, France, Portugal, Spain, US) or in some cases no use of it at all (Greece, Luxembourg) (OECD, 2008*b*; p. 15).

What are the alternatives then? Banerjee (2007, p. 21) puts the arguments in a very forceful way: "Donors are unclear about what they should be pushing for. Given that, it is easy to lead them to grandiose and unfocused project designs where none of the details are spelled out clearly and diverting money is a cinch. From this point of view, the current fashion of channelling aid into broad budgetary support (rather than specific projects) seems particularly disastrous. We need to go back to financing projects and insist that the results be measured." Arguably, however, to dichotomise the whole issue into budget support *vs.* project lending is to risk simplifying a complex question. And there

ISBN: 978-92-64-07551-1 © OECD 2009

are many intermediate aid modalities. Different aid modalities will continue to coexist. The argument here is certainly not against programme aid as a concept, simply in favour of a more cautious assessment of the implications of budget support as a "low conditionality" aid modality. There are alternatives. For instance, SWAps, where support is given for a particular sector, underpin some of the same objectives as budget support, but arguably within the more modest and achievable context of building up local capacity at a sectoral level.

Moreover, none of this implies an automatic endorsement of the current portfolio of projects. Donors have clearly promoted too many small, fragmented projects. The errors of the past need to be avoided – for example, the World Bank's increased lending orientation since the 1990s towards both huge, non-project emergency bailout packages and direct private-sector support in such areas as luxury hotels, the alcoholic beverage industry, banking, etc., all sectors with small or negligible impacts on poverty reduction. As Rich (2002, p. 26) notes, "both priorities have even less connection to directly helping the poorest of the poor than do more traditional Bank project loans". At the same time, many projects in the productive sectors remain without funding: the African-instigated New Economic Partnership for African Development (NEPAD), for example, identified many priority infrastructure projects, yet financing has often not been forthcoming[2]. The United Kingdom-led Commission for Africa (2005) suggested that Africa required an additional USD 20 billion a year in infrastructure investment, in the form of support for African regional, national, urban and rural priorities ranging from rural roads and slum upgrading to information and communication technology, and proposed that donors provide half of the additional funding up to 2010.

Regrettably, it has become much easier to mobilise resources for non-project purposes, such as technical assistance, debt relief, food aid and emergency relief, than for real development projects and programmes. In 2005, debt relief accounted for nearly one-quarter (USD 25.4 billion) of total official aid, including the Paris Club's extraordinary debt cancellation for Iraq and Nigeria. By providing funds in this fashion, donors bypass the need to have well-designed and well-implemented development projects (Kharas, 2008, p. 12). The rise in technical co-operation, the most dynamic component of spending patterns over the last 20 years, also has stemmed partly from the proliferation of ambitious new aid modalities – particularly budget support – all requiring extensive monitoring and technical capacities. In 2005, the USD 29 billion spent on technical co-operation accounted for some 40 per cent of total ODA net of debt relief and remains largely tied to expensive Northern contractors and donor control. For some recipient countries, the share went much higher. It peaked at 73 per cent in Uganda in the late 1990s (Riddell, 2007, p. 202). As much as 70 per cent of aid for education is spent on technical assistance (The Reality of Aid, 2008, p. 8). In Zambia, more money is received each year in the form of technical assistance than the whole of the government budget for education (Glennie, 2008, p. 69).

Obviously, switching back to a preference for project aid and sectoral programme support will not resolve many of the problems that afflict international aid. A real supply-side problem exists in the sheer number and diversity of new aid players, both public and private. Project aid also raises issues related to fungibility: would the funds provided for project aid really translate into increased investment in development, or would they simply allow more leeway for governments to spend more on less socially desirable goals such as military spending? But the question has equal validity for other aid modalities, and maybe is even more relevant for budget support, where oversight of government expenditures is far more onerous. While some recipient countries profess their enthusiasm for budget support, what they surely have in mind is large scale, no-strings-attached programme aid and not the kind of intrusive conditionality currently inherent in much budget and programme aid.

This is indisputably part of the reason why Chinese aid is so popular with many African governments. Arguably, the low conditionality and project-based approach of Chinese aid and the way it is linked with trade and investment policies provides some useful lessons for the donor community. Oya (2006, p. 26) is very explicit about the benefits from Chinese *vis-à-vis* OECD aid and argues that there are four potential advantages: *i)* the aid is more targeted to important infrastructure projects with long maturity and long-term potential (there is no hurry for disbursements); *ii)* it is less bureaucratic and with lower transaction costs; *iii)* it is more efficient, with lower costs and faster, and *iv)* it allows more policy space (i.e. lower conditionality) and increases the bargaining power of African countries *vis-à-vis* other donors. In fact, contrary to some reports, it is untrue that the Chinese employ no conditionality to the use of their aid, and on occasions have vigorously expressed their concerns about corruption and the possible diversion of their resources towards illegitimate uses[3].

Legitimate concerns have been raised about the appropriateness of some projects supported by Chinese financing, and whether it encourages low-income countries to take on more debt in a way which is not sustainable (Manning, 2006). The Chinese are also widely accused of turning a blind eye to human rights abuses in some African countries and of refusing to lay down governance conditions on their African trading partners. Alden (2007, p. 102) notes "the disturbing character of China's "no conditionalities" is that

ISBN: 978-92-64-07551-1 © OECD 2009

it succeeded in capturing African elites with ease, irrespective of their lack of democratic credentials. The directness of the Chinese challenge to the G8 vision for partnership and transformation is only just taking root". An alternative view is that growing Chinese engagement in Africa is laying the ground for a promising new, more workmanlike relationship between recipient governments and donors, one built on mutual respect. Chan (2008, p. 347) puts the point forcefully:

> "Africans are not naïve and should not be patronised with concerns that they are being taken for a ride. Like Hugo Chavez in Venezuela, they are rejoicing at least in having options and having suitors….The Chinese provide not only an alternative to the West but also leverage to use in continued dealings with the West. Being courted might be the prelude to being taken seriously and, in a long string of African capitals, this is the true sunrise that the Chinese bring."

Notes

1. A theoretical framework developed by Cordella and Giovanni Dell'Ariccia (2002) provides some support to this view: budget support is preferable to project aid when the preferences of donors and recipients are aligned and when assistance is small relative to the recipients' own resources. But when donors cannot observe whether the recipient government is credibly committed to developmental issues and poverty reduction programmes, the donor may find itself paradoxically imposing higher levels of conditionality in order to distinguish "committed" governments from "uncommitted" ones.

2. http://www.nepad.org/2005/files/documents/41.pdf *A Summary of NEPAD Action Plans.*

3. For instance, see Anver Versi (2006), "A Meeting of Minds and Needs", *African Business,* who discusses Chinese intervention in Angola to stop its aid money diverted to other uses.

ISBN: 978-92-64-07551-1 © OECD 2009

Chapter 8

Policy-Based Conditionality and the Economic Crisis – A Final Nail in the Coffin?

Part of the debate here might in any case be surpassed by events. As noted in the introduction to this study, prior to the crisis *de facto* power to impose conditionality via the IFIs, the custodians of the current international system of conditionality, had very much waned. The IMF in particular had seen its role very much diminished, by a combination of high commodity prices and extremely low market interest rates, giving many developing countries a degree of financial autonomy that they had not enjoyed in generations. The World Bank too had been embroiled by internal governance problems and saw the demand for its finance curtailed.

Since the final quarter of 2008, western countries have seen themselves obliged to take radical action in an attempt to stem contagion of the worst economic and financial crisis since the 1930s. Their governments have intervened massively to prop up their banking sectors, and have provided financial support to ailing industries. The irony of this has not been lost on the developing countries, who quickly remarked that the industrialised countries were now implementing measures and policies that have been prohibited to them through comprehensive conditionality for so long[1]. As a consequence, the conventional policy package is currently suffering what the German sociologist Jurgen Habermas once termed (in a different context) a "legitimation crisis".

The financial crisis provides a perhaps unique opportunity to rethink how conditionality is applied, to whom, and under what terms. Some institutions are already reacting. Under pressure to find new fast disbursing mechanisms to respond to financing difficulties created by the credit crisis, in October 2008 the IMF established a Short-Term Liquidity Facility (SLF) whereby funds are only channelled to countries the IMF considers to be "strong performers" in terms of previous reforms. This implies a kind of *ex post* conditionality, though pointedly no new conditionality is imposed on borrowers under the SLF. Second, measures of structural performance are being discontinued in all IMF arrangements, including those with low-income countries. And third, a couple of the under-utilised arrangements are to be discontinued. This is the case of the Compensatory Financing Facility, which became increasingly redundant since its modification in early 2000, which basically tightened its conditionality for access. All this is part and parcel of a wider analysis of the way in which conditionality is applied (see IMF, 2009). However key questions remain. For instance, one danger of the SLF is that the Fund is *de facto* strengthening the "eligibility" phase or criteria, whereby "stronger performers" have easier access than those who are not considered to be as such (Eurodad, 2009).

A final twist to the economic crisis is that, in a globalised economy, to paraphrase John Donne, no country is an island, and even powerful nations such as the United States find their national autonomy compromised by international finance. As a result of the enormous global imbalances generated prior to the crisis, "global liquidity is being 'sucked away' as banks in industrialised nations are bolstered by huge government infusions of funds, leaving the question of whether any cash will be left for credit and development aid needed for efforts such as achieving the Millennium Development Goals, enhancing productive capacities in poor countries, and coping with such problems there as climate change" (Supachai, 2008). After years of sustaining a level of consumption well beyond the capacity of the country to sustainably finance it, the United States in particular is likely to have increasing difficulty in attracting the necessary financial inflows. The adjustment promises to be both painful and prolonged (Wolf, 2008). Ultimately, then, all countries, rich and poor alike, find their Westphalian independence compromised to some extent through international finance, particularly in times of acute economic crisis.

The financial crisis has shown that a radical rethink of global governance is required, where responsibilities for regulation and macroeconomic adjustments are shared, much along the lines of John Maynard Keynes' thinking during the Bretton Woods negotiations in 1944[2]. It is interesting to note that in Keynes's original vision as much pressure was to be exerted on balance of payment surplus countries as for those in deficit (by way of an international tax on balance of payment surpluses at the rate of 1 per cent per month). Arguably, if the international financial architecture had been designed in this way (i.e. with mutual obligations on both deficitary and surplus countries), "conditionality" would not be perceived as being as one-sided as it is today.

ISBN: 978-92-64-07551-1 © OECD 2009

One way of operationalising this principle would be to place conditionality not only on countries that take out loans from the IMF, but also the countries which enjoy voting rights. As Prasard (2008) puts it, "the large countries routinely ignore the IMF's advice with no consequences. Economic decisions are ultimately the result of each country's political process but why should poorer countries be subject to harsher IMF scrutiny? After all, US or Chinese economic mismanagement can have much larger global consequences". Under Prasard's proposal, each country would get a list of criteria (for example, a lower budget deficit, or a more flexible exchange rate) that it would have to fulfil. There are precedents for this kind of "voluntary" self-imposed *ex ante* conditionality, such as the EU's Maastricht criteria. And it is arguably far more effective [see, for instance, Dreher (2008, pp. 38-39)]. Agreements willingly entered into are far more likely to succeed than ones that are imposed externally. That, if anything, is the major lesson to be learned from the chequered history of conditionality.

Notes

1. See, for instance, "L'Occident s'autorise ce qu'il avait interdit dans l'UMOA", *Les Afriques*, No 47: 9-15 October. Available at: www.lesafriques.com/actualite/l-occident-s-autorise-ce-qu-il-avait-interdit-dans-l-umoa.html?Itemid=89.

2. See Skidelsky (2000) for an account of these negotiations and Keynes' proposals.

ISBN: 978-92-64-07551-1 © OECD 2009

Chapter 9

Conclusions and Policy Recommendations

There is a strong sense in which the whole debate on ownership and conditionality is counterproductive and detracts attention from some serious problems which donors need to deal with urgently. The international aid architecture has grown spontaneously, and, unfortunately, suffers from major dysfunctions. Reisen (2008) describes it as a "non-system". The persistent problems which plague development assistance are well summarised in Kharas (2009). Despite the professed objective of reducing it (paragraphs 6 and 33 of the Paris Declaration), aid fragmentation is still increasing (World Bank, 2008; OECD, 2008a). There is little evidence that the administrative burden for recipient governments associated with aid delivery has decreased. Co-ordination is poor and technical assistance has grown excessively, at the expense of investment in productive and social sectors. Meanwhile, the share of country programmable aid (that is, the amount of funds available for development projects and programmes in the recipient countries) in total aid flows is still too low. These structural problems with aid delivery need urgent attention.

As Rogerson (2005, p. 550) claims, however, the real Achilles heel of the international "aid architecture" is probably the issue of conditionality: "the aid industry remains completely schizophrenic about conditionality. On the one hand, we aspire to stable long-term, predictable aid partnerships, necessary to effect the deep structural changes called for by the MDGs. But, on the other, [there is] a deep-seated need to have multiple lock-in devices that either give us the power to rescind such contracts at any time, or allow to believe we have it." Many observers lament the slow pace at which donors deliver on their commitments to reduce conditionality. The extended debates on conditionality also reflect donors' shifting perceptions regarding both the quality of democracy in developing countries and the capacity of their governments to deliver on their commitments. Despite the repetition of the word "partnership" in the

Paris Declaration, the unspoken, unpalatable truth is that donors often have little confidence in recipient governments; they have a tendency to regard aid recipients as under their tutelage. In the words of Sidney Dell (1981), they still fall into the temptation of adopting a "grandmotherly" stance.

As we have seen in Chapter 7, much empirical evidence shows that donors still broadly support allocating aid according to geostrategic priorities, political realities and historical ties. An important World Bank report (Devarajan *et al.*, 2001, p. 12) concedes that donors still use aid principally as a foreign policy tool rather than a tool for economic development. Unsurprisingly, therefore, many people in developing countries simply do not believe what they see as donor pieties about strengthening democracy and the quality of governance in developing countries through the imposition of well-defined conditions in their aid programmes. When strategic interests come into play, the western countries revert to form, it is alleged, and conveniently forget conditionality. The disconnect that often exists between government aid or development agency and other government departments with different sets of priorities compounds such problems: finance, foreign and trade ministries often call the shots, not the professionals in the aid agency. It is not immediately obvious how one can tackle this mismatch of political power or the resultant lack of coherence. In such circumstances, detailed conditionalities even on uncontroversial technical and apolitical grounds (such as controls to limit the scope for corruption) simply will not work effectively. In this study we have questioned the legitimacy of various dimensions of conditionality:

- Conditionality is contingent on political realities. Development professionals and government officials may define conditionality technically and as objectively as they can, but political realities often override their appraisals. This makes *any* elaborate system of conditionality difficult to sustain and justify. Any conditions retained should affect only policy instruments genuinely under the recipient government's control and demonstrably linked to the policy targets at which they aim.

- The evidence suggests that pushing recipient countries into adopting policies that they do not wish to adopt is neither effective nor morally defensible – it puts donors in an uncomfortable paternalistic position which most donors surely would prefer to avoid anyway.

- We have questioned the degree to which donors are capable of identifying good policies. Especially in the light of the financial crisis, it would seem that a more unassuming approach towards relations with the developing world would be merited. The industrialised countries clearly do not have

ISBN: 978-92-64-07551-1 © OECD 2009

all the answers regarding the design and application of policy, especially in social, cultural and political contexts in which they are not familiar.

- Constantly shifting donor positions and an apparently low capacity within the donor community to maintain the momentum of initiatives make it very difficult for any developing country to keep up with, let alone implement, policies. Low degrees of compliance with conditionality are hardly surprising in such circumstances.

- Any aid modality which involves selecting appropriate recipients on the basis of past performance (*ex post* conditionality) risks marginalising the poorest and most needy developing countries, making it a criterion which is difficult to justify or defend. Some kind of selection process by donors is of course inevitable – there are simply too many unmet needs requiring attention – but explicit *ex post* criteria must be used sparingly if at all.

- In an ideal world, budget support and outcome-based conditionality focused particularly on social goals, as currently embraced by donors such as the EC, the Netherlands and the United Kingdom, might well be desirable. But in practice there are many complications to implementing such an approach. Again, political realities both in the recipient and donor countries circumvent technical assessments of compliance and make such ambitious systems of aid disbursement and conditionality untenable in many cases.

- Finally, it is clear that *policy space* for developing countries in many spheres has shrunk quite dramatically over the last three decades. This is not due to donor policies alone, but rather a gradual process by private and public interests of "hemming in" the viable options open to developing countries through bodies like the World Trade Organization. Against this backdrop, this study reiterates the need for more "policy space" for aid recipients in order to be able to elaborate efficient strategies and policies for development. Defining exactly how to achieve this is regrettably beyond the scope of the current study[1]. But it is clear that a major cutback in conditionality is a *sine qua non* condition to achieving that objective.

Nevertheless, one risks throwing out the baby with the bathwater in sweeping criticisms of conditionality. These arguments do not mean that conditionality in any shape or form is unwarranted. In particular circumstances it will always be required:

- When a recipient government clearly abuses *human rights* and/or its commitment to poverty reduction is questionable, the donor community needs to act boldly, making greater efforts to ensure that its members work in unison on these issues. Here the goal of donor alignment in the Paris Declaration comes into its own. For example, the reaction of the donor community to the troubles surrounding the 2007 Kenyan elections showed how, when acting together, external political pressure can help avert disaster.

- *Fiduciary conditionality* is of upmost importance in maintaining the credibility of the aid system. Donors have a responsibility to ensure that taxpayers' money is spent appropriately, i.e. for development purposes. Yet it is worth recognising explicitly and openly that donors have not always done their best to limit corruption and reduce the diversion of aid flows to illicit uses: pressure on aid agencies and IFIs to disburse funds often overrides concerns regarding fiduciary accountability. The results are satisfactory for no one.

To sum up, what would a positive agenda for reform on aid conditionality look like? Here we provide a few final pointers, suggestions and observations:

- The word "ownership" needs much more sparing and prudent use than over the last decade. We believe Buiter (2004) is right when he says "the concept of 'country ownership' has been used and abused in so many ways that it now is at best unhelpful and at worst misleading and obfuscating." Donors in particular need to avoid the temptation of only viewing local ownership as 'good' when countries follow the donor's script[2]. If donors are serious about ownership, taking strong positions on national policies should be avoided. Adopting what Kanbur (2000, p. 10) calls a more "arms-length relationship" with recipients would represent a better strategy.

- Convincing development partners through argument rather than obliging them to through conditionality is surely a better way forward. Donors need to avoid at all costs pushing their own ideas on recipient countries. This is especially true in the wake of a financial crisis which has exposed serious fault lines in certain dimensions of mainstream policy advice (e.g. on financial liberalisation and deregulation). Building mutual consensus between donors and recipients around some simple themes is a good approach, such as the 20-20 Initiative proposed at the Copenhagen Social Summit in 1995, which obliged *both* donors and developing country governments to dedicate at least 20 per cent of their budgets to basic social services. It is regrettable that initiatives like this one have never been followed through sufficiently.

ISBN: 978-92-64-07551-1 © OECD 2009

- Aid recipients themselves have a responsibility to take the initiative and seize their own policy space. Some countries have managed greater autonomy, simply by dint of avoiding entanglements through excessive levels of debt, for example. A few authors (e.g. Whitfield and Fraser, 2009) now speak of the importance of imposing a kind of "reverse conditionality" whereby aid-receiving countries would set conditions on *donors* in order to enhance the quality of aid. Recipients would, in other words, become more "choosy" about the kind of aid they accept. For very poor countries, such a strategy might be difficult to put in practice. But given the slow pace of implementation of the Paris Declaration on the part of the donor community, there are surely some merits in recipients themselves adopting a more proactive approach in their relations with donors.

- Imaginative ways do exist in which to minimise or at least reduce conditionality, simply by shifting the modality of aid delivery. Over the last decade or two, donors have channelled aid disproportionately towards technical support to the detriment of investment in productive sectors (UNCTAD, 2008). In their enthusiasm for new, quick disbursing aid modalities (above all, budget support), they have overlooked some of the virtues of project aid. This needs rectifying. In this context, the low conditionality project-based approach of Chinese aid and the way it is linked with trade and investment policies provides some useful lessons for the donor community.

- The comprehensive nature of conditionality smacks of social engineering in many of the most ambitious donor programmes. Yet as Easterly (2006, p. 322) notes, "the aim should be to make individuals better off, not to transform governments or societies. Once the West is willing to aid individuals rather than governments, some conundrums that tie foreign aid up in knots are resolved". For example, donors can support schemes that provide direct income support through transfers to the poor (Hanlon, 2004; Holmqvist, 2008). Schemes have been implemented in Latin America providing child allowances conditional on school attendance and vaccination. Welfare schemes for the elderly have been started in India, Lesotho and South Africa. More donor support for such schemes would help promote the incipient movement towards social protection as a *right* in developing countries, rather than as beneficiaries of aid[3].

- Valuable lessons can be learned from the past. For example, the EC's approach to development co-operation with the African, Caribbean and Pacific (ACP) countries under the Lomé Convention was arguably one of the most even-handed arrangements between a group of developing

ISBN: 978-92-64-07551-1 © OECD 2009

and industrialised countries. It combined trade and aid aspects, and the pronounced emphasis on equality between Southern and Northern partners resulted in an unprecedented, strong Southern-country position (Singer and Raffer, 1996, p. 88). It introduced compensatory payments for fluctuations in export earnings of some commodities (the STABEX scheme) as a contractual right of ACP countries, very much like insurance payments. Unfortunately, the EC itself gradually undermined the arrangement, as it encountered budgetary constraints on honouring its commitments and as the temptation to make transfers increasingly conditional proved too great to resist. Regardless of whether one agrees or not with the central role assigned to budget support, the EC's MDG contracts, whereby donor commitments are made explicit and monitoring is focused principally on indicators of health and education, represents an important step in recovering that earlier kind of stance regarding mutual commitments.

- Some smaller DAC donors provide useful insights on conditionality and sometimes lessons about how it can go awry. Forster (1995) notes that the whole the concept of development adopted by the Swiss government, with regard to its interpretation of good governance and the values upon which its human-rights policy is based, differ little from those of other European powers. Yet Switzerland has been reluctant to use development co-operation through conditionality to put pressure on recipient countries. On occasions, such a stance has attracted vehement criticism, as in the 1980s when the Swiss government continued to provide aid to Nicaragua, despite American pressures to do otherwise. This Swiss "exceptionalism" stems in part from the small size and power of the country, so that it does not feel in a position to set conditions for development assistance. But it also derives from the historic Swiss "principle of non-interference" in domestic affairs of other countries. It would be a good principle for other larger donors to emulate[4].

- Given the scale of the current credit crisis and the global imbalances which underlie the international financial system, it would seem apparent that rich countries also require some form of external discipline (conditionality) themselves in making the necessary macroeconomic adjustments. One way of operationalising this principle would be to place conditionality not only on countries that take out loans from the IMF, but also the countries which enjoy voting rights (Prasard, 2008). Each country would get a list of criteria (for example, a lower current account imbalance, or a more flexible exchange rate) that it would have to fulfil. There are precedents for this kind of "voluntary" self-imposed *ex ante* conditionality, such as

ISBN: 978-92-64-07551-1 © OECD 2009

the EU's Maastricht criteria. Conditionality within such a framework basis would certainly carry more legitimacy within the developing world. Conditionality should no longer be a one-way street.

Finally, a lot is at stake for the donor community. A number of highly critical studies have recently been released on international aid (Glennie, 2008; Tandon, 2008; Moyo, 2009; Wrong, 2009). The Rwandan government has recently announced that it is exploring ways of ending aid dependence. Criticisms of the international aid architecture are thus gaining momentum. Conditionality remains one of the major bones of contention between donors and recipients. The recent financial crisis has magnified those long-standing grievances. The problem of conditionality needs to be dealt with in a more serious, transparent and even-handed manner than it has in the past. It would be reckless for the donor community to ignore these warning signs.

Notes

1. See, for instance, Gallagher (2005) and Chang (2005).

2. For instance, in Ethiopia political motivations lie behind government reticence to allow land reform (all land ownership is retained by the state). Political realities therefore dictate the extent to which the Ethiopian government is prepared to go with reform. Are such limits justified? Any true believer in ownership would have to concede "Yes", even though some of these reforms might be highly desirable for the mass of poor people in Ethiopia.

3. For an examination of some of the issues involved, see Mold (1998).

4. In the 1970s and early 1980s, the Swedish co-operation agency SIDA adopted a similar policy of respecting recipient nations' sovereignty and recipient-led strengthening of their public sectors. In the mid-1980s, however, Sweden's domestic economy dipped and a stronger pro-business mood emerged. Sweden began to sing in "the one-note choir of donor voices" (Sogge, 2002, pp. 78-79).

ISBN: 978-92-64-07551-1 © OECD 2009

References

ActionAid (2005), "International Submission on the World Bank Review of Conditionality", 28 June 2005. Available at http://siteresources.worldbank.org/PROJECTS/578280-1119562936151/20571579/WBconditionalityreviewcommentsAAJune05.pdf

Afrodad (2006), "Assessing the Impact of the PRGF on Social Services in Selected African Countries: A Synthesis Report on Ethiopia, Malawi, Zambia and the United Republic of Tanzania", African Forum and Network on Debt and Development, Harare.

Alden, C. (2007), *China in Africa*, Zed Books, London.

Alesina, A. and B. Weder (2002), "Do Corrupt Governments Receive Less Foreign Aid?", *American Economic Review*, Vol. 92, No. 4. pp. 1126-1137.

Andersen, T., T.H. Barneck and F. Tarp (2006), "On US Politics and IMF Lending", *European Economic Review*, Vol. 50, No. 7, pp. 1843–1862.

Ardnt, C. and C. Oman (2006), *Uses and Abuses of Government Indicators*, Development Centre Studies, OECD Development Centre, Paris.

AusAid (2003), "The Contribution of Australian Aid to Papua New Guinea's Development 1975–2000: Provisional Conclusions from a Rapid Assessment", *Evaluation and Review Series*, No. 34, June.

Banerjee, A.V. (2007), "Making Aid Work", *Boston Review*, MIT Press.

Baylies, C. (1995), "'Political Conditionality' and Democratisation", *Review of African Political Economy*, No. 65, pp. 321-337.

Berthélemy, J.-C. (2006), "Bilateral Donors' Interest vs. Recipients, Development Motives in Aid Allocation: Do All Donors Behave the Same?", *Review of Development Economics*, Vol. 10, No. 2, pp. 179-194.

Bird, G. (1985), "Relationships, Resource Uses and the Conditionality Debate", *in* T. Killick and G.R. Bird (eds.), *The Quest for Economic Stabilization – The IMF and the Third World*, Gower/ODI, Aldershot, pp. 145-182.

Bissio, R. (2008), "The Paris Declaration Does Not Go Far Enough", *in The Reality of Aid (2008), Aid Effectiveness: "Democratic Ownership and Human Rights"*, Ibon Books, Quezon City Philippines, pp. 126-134. Available at: http://realityofaid.org/downloads/RoAReports2008_full.pdf

Browne, S. (2007), *Aid and Influence – Do Donors Help or Hinder?*, Earthscan, London.

Buira, A. (2003), "An Analysis of IMF Conditionality", *in* A. Buira and D. Rodrik (ed.), *Challenges to the World Bank and IMF – Developing Country Perspectives*, Anthem Press, London.

Buiter, W. (2004), "Country Ownership: a Term Whose Time Has Gone". Available at: www.nber.org/~wbuiter/condition.pdf.

Burnside, C. and D. Dollar (2000), "Aid, Policies and Growth", *The American Economic Review*, Vol. 90, No. 4, pp. 847-868.

Calderisi, R. (2007), *The Trouble with Africa – Why Foreign Aid isn´t Working*, Yale University Press.

Caulfield, C. (1996), *Masters of Illusion – the World Bank and the Poverty of Nations*, Pan Books, London.

Chambers, R. (2005), *Ideas for Development*, Earthscan, London.

Chan, S. (2008), "Ten Caveats and One Sunrise in our Contemplation of China and Africa", *in* C. Alden, D. Large and R. Soares de Oliveira (eds), *China Returns to Africa – A Rising Power and a Continent Embrace, Hurst and Company*, London, pp. 339-347.

Chang, H.-J. (2005), "Policy Space in Historical Perspective – With Special Reference to Trade and Industrial Policies", paper presented at the Queen Elizabeth House 50th Anniversary Conference,"The Development Threats and Promises", Queen Elizabeth House, University of Oxford, 4-5 July, www.qeh.ox.ac.uk/dissemination/conference-papers/chang.pdf.

Collier, P. (2006), "Is Aid Oil? An Analysis of Whether Africa Can Absorb More Aid", *World Development*, Vol. 34, No. 9, pp. 1482–1497.

Commission for Africa (2005), *Our Common Interest – An Argument*, Penguin Books, London.

Committee of Public Accounts (2008), Department for International Development: Providing budget support for developing countries: Twenty–seventh Report of Session 2007–08, House of Commons, www.publications.parliament.uk/pa/cm200708/cmselect/cmpubacc/395/395.pdf

Cordella, T. and G. Dell'ariccia (2002), "Limits of Conditionality in Poverty Reduction Programs", *IMF Staff Papers*, Vol. 49.

Cortright, D. and A. Lopez (2000), *The Sanctions Decade: Assessing UN Strategies in the 1990s*, Lynne Rienner, Boulder, Colorado.

Crawford, M. (1983), "High Conditionality Lending: The United Kingdom", *in* J. Williamson (ed.), *IMF Conditionality, Institute for International Economics*, Washington, D.C., pp.421-439.

Davis, L. and S. Engerman (2003), "History Lessons: Sanctions: Neither War nor Peace", *The Journal of Economic Perspectives*, Vol. 17, No. 2, spring, pp. 187-197.

ISBN: 978-92-64-07551-1 © OECD 2009

DEATON, A., A. BANERJEE, N. LUSTIG and K. ROGOFF (2006), "An Evaluation of World Bank Research 1998-2005", World Bank, Washington, D.C., September.

DELL, S. (1981), "On Being Grandmotherly: The Evolution of IMF Conditionality", *Princeton University Essays in International Finance*, No. 144, October.

DEVARAJAN S., D.R. DOLLAR and T. HOLMGREN (eds.) (2001), *Aid and Reform in Africa*, World Bank, Washington D.C.

DFID (2005), "Partnership for Poverty Reduction: Rethinking Conditionality – A UK policy paper", March. Available at: www.dfid.gov.uk/Documents/publications/conditionality.pdf.

DOLLAR, D. and J. SVENSSON (2000), "What Explains the Success or Failure of Structural Adjustment Programmes", *The Economic Journal*, Vol. 110, No. 466, pp. 894-917.

DRAZEN, A. and P. ISARD (2004), "Can Public Discussion Enhance Program Ownership?", *NBER Working Papers No. 10927*, National Bureau of Economic Research, Inc., New York, NY.

DREHER, A. (2006), "IMF and Economic Growth: The Effects of Programs, Loans and Compliance with Conditionality", *World Development*, Vol. 34, No. 5, pp. 769-788.

DREHER, A. (2008), "IMF Conditionality – Theory and Evidence", *Working Papers* No. 188, KOF Swiss Economic Institute, ETH Zurich, February.

EASTERLY, W. (2003), "Can Foreign Aid Buy Growth?", *Journal of Economic Perspectives*, Vol. 17, No. 3, summer, pp. 23–48.

EASTERLY, W. (2006), *The White Man's Burden – Why the West's Efforts to Aid the Rest have Done So Much Ill and So Little Good*, Penguin Press, New York, NY.

EASTERLY, W. (2007), "Are Aid Agencies Improving?", *Economic Policy*, October, pp. 634-678.

EDWARDS, M.S. (1999), *Future Positive – International Co-operation in the 21st Century*, Earthscan, London.

EDWARDS, M.S. (2001), "Crime and Punishment: Understanding IMF Sanctioning Practices", mimeo, Rutgers University.

EUROPEAN COMMISSION (2005), *EC Budget Support: An Innovative Approach to Conditionality*, Economic Commission, Brussels, February.

EURODAD (2007), "Untying the Knots – How the World Bank is Failing to Deliver Real Change on Conditionality", *Eurodad report*. Available at: www.eurodad.org/whatsnew/reports.aspx?id=1804.

EURODAD (2008), "Outcome-based Conditonality: Too Good to Be True?", *Eurodad report*, February. Available at: www.eurodad.org/uploadedFiles/Whats_New/Reports/Outcome_based_conditionality.pdf

EURODAD (2009), "Partial Victory: The IMF Abolishes One Conditionality Type," 27 March 2009. Available at: www.eurodad.org/whatsnew/articles.aspx?id=3502

FELDSTEIN, M. (1998), "Refocusing the IMF", *Foreign Affairs*, Vol. 77, No. 2.

FORSTER, J. (1995), "Conditionality in Swiss Development Assistance", *in* O. STOKKE (ed.) *Aid and Political Conditionality*, Frank Cass, London.

FREY, B. and R. EICHENBERGER (1994), "The Political Economy of Stabilization Programmes in Developing Countries", *European Journal of Political Economy*, Vol. 10, No.1, pp. 169-190.

GALLAGHER, K.P. (ed.) (2005), *Putting Development First – The Importance of Policy Space in the WTO and International Financial Institution*, Zed Books, London.

GLENNIE, G. (2008), *The Trouble with Aid – Why Less Could Mean More for Africa*, Zed Books, London.

HALL, D. and R. DE LA MOTTE (2004), "Dogmatic Development: Privatisation and Conditionalities in Six Countries", a PSIRU report for War on Want. Available at: www.psiru.org/reports/2004-02-U-condits.pdf.

HANSEN, H. and TARP, F. (2001), "Aid and Growth Regressions", *Journal of Development Economics*, Vol. 64, No. 2, April, pp. 547-570.

HANLON, J. (2004), "Is It Possible to Just Give Money to the Poor?", *Development and Change*, Vol. 35, No. 2, April.

HIRSCHMAN, A.O. (1987), "On the Political Economy of Latin America", *in* A.O. HIRSCHMAN (1995), *A Propensity to Self-Subversion*, Harvard University Press, Cambridge.

HOLMQVIST, G. (2008), "The Case for Cash Aid to Africans – Not to Their Governments", *Europe's World*, summer 2008, No. 9, pp.180-187.

IDA (2003), "Allocating IDA Funds Based on Performance. Fourth Annual Report on IDA's Country Assessment and Allocation Process", http://siteresources.worldbank.org/IDA/Resources/PBAAR4.pdf

IDD and ASSOCIATES (2006), *Evaluation of General Budget Support: Synthesis Report,* Available at: www.oecd.org/dataoecd/42/38/36685401.pdf.

IMF and WORLD BANK (2001), *Poverty Reduction Strategy Papers – Progress in Implementation,* Washington, D.C., September.

IMF (2007), "An IEO Evaluation of Structural Conditionality in IMF-Supported Programs", Independent Evaluation Office, International Monetary Fund, Washington, D.C., 27 November.

IMF (2009), "IMF Implements Major Lending Policy Improvements", Press Release, 24 March 2009, www.imf.org/external/np/pdr/fac/2009/032409.htm.

ISBN: 978-92-64-07551-1 © OECD 2009

Joyce, J.P. (2006), "Promises Made, Promises Broken: A Model of IMF Program Implementation", *Economics and Politics*, Vol. 18, No. 3, pp. 339-365.

Kanbur, R. (2000), "Aid, Conditionality and Debt in Africa", *in* F. Tarp (ed.), *Foreign Aid and Development – Lessons Learnt and Directions for the Future*, Routledge, London, pp. 409-422.

Kharas, H. (2008), "Trends and Issues in Development Aid", Brookings Institution, Available at: www.brookings.edu/papers/2007/11_development_aid_kharas.aspx

Kharas, H. (2009), "Action on Aid: Steps Toward Making Aid More Effective", Brookings Institution, Available at: www.brookings.edu/reports/2009/04_aid_kharas.aspx

Killick, T. (ed.) (1985), *The Quest for Economic Stabilisation – the IMF and the Third World*, Gower, London.

Killick, T. (2005), "Did Conditionality Streamlining Succeed?" *in* S. Koeberle, H. Bedoya, P. Silarsky and G. Verheyen (eds), Conditionality Revisited – Concepts, Experiences and Lessons, World Bank, Washington, D.C.

Killick, T. (2008), "Taking Control: Aid Management Policies in Least Developed Countries", background paper for the UNCTAD *The Least Developed Countries Report Growth, Poverty and Terms of Development Partnership 2008*. Available at: www.unctad.org/sections/ldc_dir/docs/ldcr2008_Killick_en.pdf.

Killick, T. (with R. Gunatilakia and A. Marr) (1998), *Aid and the Political Economy of Policy Change*, Routledge/ODI, London.

Killick, T. and D. Lawson, (2007), "Budget Support to Ghana: A Risk Worth Taking?", *ODI Briefing Paper* No. 24, Overseas Development Institute, London, July.

Kindleberger, C. and R.Z. Aliber (2005), *Manias, Panics and Crashes – A History of Financial Crises* (fifth edition), Basingstoke; Palgrave MacMillan.

Knoll, M. (2008), "Budget Support: A Reformed Approach or Old Wine In New Skins?", UNCTAD, Geneva.

Kohli, A. (2004), *State-Directed Development – Political Power and Industrialisation in the Global Periphery*, Cambridge University Press, Cambridge.

Krasner, S (1999), *Sovereignty: Organized Hypocrisy*, Princeton University Press, Princeton, NJ.

Lancaster, C. (2007), *Foreign Aid – Diplomacy, Development, Domestic Politics*, The University of Chicago Press, Chicago.

Lensink, R. and O. Morrissey (1999), "Aid Instability as a Measure of Uncertainty and the Positive Impact of Aid on Growth," CDS Research Reports No. 199906, University of Groningen, Centre for Development Studies (CDS).

Manning, R. (2006), "Will 'Emerging Donors' Change the Face of International Co-operation?", *Development Policy Review*, Vol, 24, No. 4, pp.371-385.

McGilligray, M. and O. Morrissey (1999), "Evaluating Economic Liberalization", *Case Studies in Economic Development*, Vol. 4, Palgrave Macmillan, London.

McGilligray, M., S. Feeny, N. Hermes and R. Lensink (2006), "Controversies over the Impact of Development Aid: It works, It Doesn't; It Can, but that Depends...", *Journal of International Development*, Vol. 18, No. 7, pp. 1031-1050.

Mecagni, M. (1999) "The Causes of Program Interruptions", *in* Bredenkamp H. and S. Schadler (eds), *Economic Adjustment and Reform in Low-Income Countries*, International Monetary Fund, Washington, D.C.

Mold, A. (1998) (ed.), *Public Policy and Children*, UNICEF, TACRO, Bogota.

Mold, A. (2007), *EU Development Policy in a Changing World – Challenges for the 21st Century*, Amsterdam University Press, Amsterdam.

Morrissey, O. (2001), "Pro-Poor Conditionality for Aid and Debt Relief in East Africa", CREDIT Research Paper No. 15. Available at: www.nottingham.ac.uk/economics/credit/research/papers/CP.01.15.PDF.

Mosley, P. (1987) "Conditionality as a Bargaining Process: Structural-Adjustment Lending, 1980-86", *Essays in International Finance*, No. 168, October.

Mosley, P. and M.J. Eeckhout (2000) "From Project Aid to Programme Assistance", *in* Tarp, F. and P. Hjertholm (eds.), *Foreign Aid and Development: Lessons Learnt and Directions for the Future*, Routledge, New York, NY.

Mosley, P., J. Harrigan and J. Toye (1991), *Aid and Power, the World Bank and Policy-based Lending*, Vol. 1, Routledge, London.

Mosley, P., J. Hudson and A. Verschoor (2004), "Aid, Poverty Reduction and the 'New Conditionality'", *The Economic Journal*, Vol. 114, No. 496, pp. 217-243.

Moyo, D. (2009), *Dead Aid – Why Aid is Not Working and How there is Another Way for Africa*, Allen Lane, London.

Nolan, P. (2004), *Transforming China – Globalisation, Transition and Development*, Anthem Press, London.

Noorbakhsh, F. and A. Paloni (2001), "Structural Adjustment and Growth in Sub-Saharan Africa: The Importance of Complying with Conditionality", *Economic Development and Cultural Change*, Vol. 49, No. 3, pp. 479-509.

OECD (1991), *Principles for Programme Assistance*, OECD, Paris.

OECD (1996), *OECD Shaping the 21st Century*, OECD, Paris.

OECD (2005), *Paris Declaration on Aid Effectiveness. Ownership, Harmonisation, Alignment, Results and Mutual Accountability*, OECD, Paris.

OECD (2008*a*), "Scaling up: Aid Fragmentation, Aid Allocation and Aid Predictability – Report of 2008 Survey of Aid Allocation Policies and Indicative Forward Spending Plans", May. Available at: www.oecd.org/dac/scalingup.

ISBN: 978-92-64-07551-1 © OECD 2009

OECD (2008*b*), "Implementing the Paris Declaration: Lessons from Peer Reviews – Synthesis Report", DCD/DAC(2008)17/REV1.

OYA, C. (2006), "The Political Economy of Development Aid as Main Source of Foreign Finance for Poor African Countries: Loss of Policy Space and Possible Alternatives from East Asia", Paper presented at the Second Annual Conference of the International Forum on the Comparative Political Economy of Globalisation, 1-3 September, Renmin University of China, Beijing, China.

PINCUS, J. and J. WINTERS (2002), *Reinventing the World Bank*, Cornell University Press.

POLAK, J.J. (1991), "The Changing Nature of IMF Conditionality", *Working Paper* No. 41, OECD Development Centre, Paris

PRASARD, E. (2008), "No More Tinkering at the IMF", *The Financial Times*, 3 November.

PRITCHETT, L. and M. WOOLCOCK (2004), "Solutions when the Solution is the Problem: Arraying the Disarray in Development', *World Development*, Vol 32, No. 2, pp.191-212.

THE REALITY OF AID (2008), *Aid Effectiveness: Democratic Ownership and Human Rights*, Ibon Books, Quezon City Philippines. Available at: http://realityofaid.org/downloads/RoAReports2008_full.pdf.

REINHART, C.M. and K.S. ROGOFF (2008), "This Time is Different: A Panoramic View of Eight Centuries of Financial Crises", *NBER Working Papers* 13882, National Bureau of Economic Research, Inc.

REISEN, H. (2008), "Ownership in the Multilateral Development-Finance Non-System", *in Financing Development 2008 – Whose Ownership?*, OECD Development Centre, Paris.

RENZIO, P., DE (2006), "Aid, Budgets and Accountability: A Survey Article", *Development Policy Review*, Vol. 24, No. 6, pp. 627-645.

RENZIO, P., DE and J. HANLON (2009), "Mozambique: Contested Sovereignty? The Dilemmas of Aid Dependence", *in* L.WHITFIELD (2009) (ed.), *The Politics of Aid – African Strategies for Dealing with Donors*, Oxford University Press, pp. 246-270.

RICH, B. (2002) "The World Bank under James Wolfensohn" by J. PINCUS and J. WINTERS (eds.), *Reinventing the World Bank*, Cornell University Press, pp. 26-53

RIDDELL, R. (2007), *Does Foreign Aid Really Work?*, Oxford University Press.

RODRIK, D. (2006). "Goodbye Washington Consensus, Hello Washington Confusion? A Review of the World Bank's, Economic Growth in the 1990s: Learning from a Decade of Reform", *Journal of Economic Literature*, Vol. 44, No.4, pp. 973-987, American Economic Association, December.

RODRIK, D. (2007), *One Economics, Many Recipes – Globalisation, Institutions and Economic Growth*, Princeton University Press, Princeton, NJ.

ROGERSON, A. (2005), "Aid Harmonisation and Alignment: Bridging the Gaps Between Reality and the Paris Reform Agenda", *Development Policy Review,* Vol. 23, No. 5, pp. 531-552, September.

SCHMITZ, A. (2006), "Conditionality in Development Aid Policy", *SWP Research Paper,* No. 7, Berlin.

SENDER, J. (2002), "Reassessing the Role of the World Bank in Sub-Saharan Africa", *in* PINCUS and WINTERS *(op. cit.)*, pp.185-202.

SINGER, H.W. and K. RAFFER (1996), *The Foreign Aid Business. Economic Assistance and Development Co-operation,* Edward Elgar, Cheltenham, UK and Brookfield, US.

SKIDELSKY, R. (2000), *John Maynard Keynes: Fighting for Britain 1937-1946,* Papermac, London.

SOGGE, D. (2002), *Give and Take – What's the Matter with Foreign Aid?,* Zed Books, London.

STEWART, F. and M. WANG (2003), "Do PRSPs Empower Poor Countries and Disempower the World Bank or is it the Other Way Round?", *QEH Working Paper,* No. 108, Queen Elizabeth House, University of Oxford, Oxford.

STIGLITZ, J. (2005), "Post-Washington Consensus" *Initiative for Policy Dialogue Working Paper Series,* Columbia University, New York, NY.

STOLTENBERG, T. (1989), "Towards a Development Strategy?", *in* L. EMMERIJ (ed), *One World or Several?* Development Centre Studies, OECD, Paris, pp. 107-119.

STREETEN, P. (1988), "Conditionality: A Double Paradox", *in* C.J. JEPMA (ed.), *North-South Co-operation in Retrospect and Prospect,* Routledge, London, pp.107-119.

SUPACHAI P. (2008), "UNCTAD Officials Say UN Should be Involved, All Countries' Interests Reflected in Response to Financial Crisis", Press Release, UNCTAD/ PRESS/PR/2008/042, 16/10/08. Available at: www.unctad.org/Templates/webflyer. asp?docid=10721&intItemID=4697&lang=1

SVENSSON, J. (2000), "Foreign Aid and Rent-Seeking", *Journal of International Economics,* Vol. 51, No. 2 pp. 437-461.

TANDON, Y. (2008), *Ending Aid Dependence, Fahamu and the South Centre,* Geneva.

TARP, F. (2001), Book Review of "Aid and Reform in Africa" by S. DEVARAJAN, D. DOLLAR and T. HOLMGREN, World Bank, 2000, *Journal of African Economies,* Vol. 10, No. 3, pp. 341–53.

TOYE, J. (1993), *Dilemmas of Development* (second edition), Blackwell, Oxford.

TOYE, J. and R. TOYE (2004), *The UN and Global Political Economy: Trade, Finance and Development,* Indiana University Press, Bloomington.

UNCTAD (2008) *Trade and Development Report, 2008 – Commodity Prices, Capital Flows and The Financing of Investment,* United Nations, New York and Geneva.

Versi, A. (2006), "A Meeting of Minds and Needs", *African Business*, n° 322, July.

White, H.N. and A.G. Dijkstra (2003), Programme Aid and Development Beyond Conditionality, *Routledge Studies in Development Economics* No. 29, Routledge, London/New York.

Whitfield, L. and A. Fraser (2009), "Introduction: Aid and Sovereignty" *in* Whitfield, L. (ed.), *The Politics of Aid – African Strategies for Dealing with Donors*, Oxford University Press, pp. 1-26.

Whitfield, L. and G. Maipose, (2008), "Managing Aid Dependence: How African Governments Lost Ownership and How They Can Regain it", *Global Economic Governance Programme*, University College, Oxford.

Williamson, J. (ed.) (1983), *IMF Conditionality*, Institute for International Economics, Washington, D.C.

Winters, J. (2002), "Criminal Debt", *in* Pincus and Winters (*op. cit.*), pp. 101-130.

Wolf, M. (2008a), "The World Wakes from the Wish-Dream of Decoupling", *The Financial Times*, 21 October.

Wolf, M. (2008b), "Fixing Global Finance – How to Curb Financial Crises in the 21st Century", Yale University Press, London.

Woods, N. (2007), "The Shifting Politics of Foreign Aid", *Global Economic Governance Programme Working Paper* No. 36, University College Oxford.

World Bank (1992), Effective Implementation: Key to Development Impact, Report of the Portfolio Management Task Force (Wapenhams Report), World Bank, Washington, D.C.

World Bank (1998), "Assessing Aid: What Works, What Doesn't and Why", *World Bank Policy Research Report*, Oxford University Press, New York, NY.

World Bank (2005), *Review of World Bank Conditionality, Operations Policy and Country Services*, World Bank, Washington, D.C.

World Bank (2007), "Conditionality in Development Policy Lending", Operations Policy and Country Services, 15 November, Washington, D.C.

World Bank (2008), *Global Monitoring Report 2008, MDGs and the Environment: Agenda for Inclusive and Sustainable Development*, World Bank, Washington, D.C.

Wrong, M. (2002), *In the Footsteps of Mr. Kurtz: Living on the Brink of Disaster in Mobutu's Congo*, Harper Perennial, New York, NY.

Wrong, M. (2009), *It's Our Turn to Eat: The Story of a Kenyan Whistle Blower*, Fourth Estate, London.

Zimmermann, F. and I. McDonnell (2008), "Broader Ownership for Development", *in Financing Development 2008 – Whose Ownership?*, OECD Development Centre, Paris.

OECD PUBLISHING, 2, rue André-Pascal, 75775 PARIS CEDEX 16
PRINTED IN FRANCE
(41 2009 04 1 P) OISBN 978-92-64-07551-1 – No. 56961 2009